We Work with HORSES

TRAINER · GROOM · JOCKEY · HOTWALKER · INSTRUCTOR
BLACKSMITH · VETERINARIAN · SHOW RIDER · BREEDER

by Patrice Clay

G.P. PUTNAM'S SONS · NEW YORK

All photos are by the author with the exception
of the following: p. 2: Bruce Curtis, pp. 68, 74:
Fallaw; p. 117: UPI, p. 136: KEEP.

Library of Congress Cataloging in Publication Data
Clay, Patrice A.
We work with horses.
Includes index.
SUMMARY: Describes a variety of jobs in the
horse industry, including show rider, farrier,
veterinarian assistant, jockey, and rodeo rider.
1. Horse industry—Vocational guidance—
Juvenile literature. [1. Horse industry—
Vocational guidance—Juvenile literature.
2. Vocational guidance] I. Title
SF285.25.C52   1980   636.1'0023   80-18319
ISBN 0-399-20735-X

Contents

Introduction

The horse population is growing at a full gallop. The American Horse Council estimates that there are 9 million horses in the United States today—more than there were at the turn of the century when they were necessary for transportation, and twice as many as in 1960. The huge racing industry and over 3 million pleasure horse owners are the reasons for this upsurge.

It takes a lot of people to keep the horse industry going. And it is an industry. Over the past twenty years the horse business, which includes everything from mane-stiffening sprays to electric fire alarms for stalls, has grown as much as any other business in this country. The job opportunities within it are numerous and some are highly profitable.

Many young people who fall in love with horses can imagine no better way to earn a living than by working with these magnificent animals. But it takes more than a love for horses to be successful in the business, as any experienced horse person will tell you.

You must be willing to put up with the long hours, aching muscles, and low pay that are part of most beginner-level jobs. With the exception of a few highly trained people such as veterinarians, almost everyone starts at the bottom, mucking out stalls, grooming horses, and cleaning tack. How much money you make depends on a lot of variables—what you do, where you work, for whom you work, and how good you are at your job. Many I talked to reported low salaries, but those who rise toward the top do earn a comfortable living.

Most job opportunities lie in riding instruction and stable management, training and breeding. But as you will see in the following chapters there is a full gamut of possibilities: show rider, farrier (blacksmith), veterinarian assistant, jockey, and even rodeo rider.

1
Hotwalker

At 9:00 A.M. it was late in the day for New York's Belmont racetrack. Rub rags and horse bandages hung from clotheslines strung behind the barns in the hazy morning sunlight.

I was being escorted around the barn area by Lt. Bob Skelly, a veteran of twenty-five years on the New York City police force who is now in charge of the Belmont security force. I was amazed by the size and complexity of the backstretch. To racing fans the term "backstretch" refers to the area of the track farthest from the grandstand and opposite to the homestretch. But to those who work behind the scenes, backstretch is a general term that encompasses the entire barn area. The Belmont backstretch is made up of 457 acres on which there are sixty-three barns that house some 2,400 racehorses. About 1,200 people work there and many of them live in dorms in the track compound. The compound itself is like a mini-city with its own post office, security guards and police force, fire fighters, ambulances, restaurants, and houses.

It also has its own rules and etiquette, all of which revolve around the valuable racehorses. When you drive through the backstretch there are security guards and posted signs at every corner and intersection to stop traffic and let the racehorses through on their way to and from the track. You quickly learn to watch out for the horses. I couldn't even contemplate the disgrace of being accused of threatening one with reckless driving.

Lt. Skelly gave me a quick guided tour so I would be able to make my way back to the main gate through the maze of barns. Armed with a set of instructions and a round of introductions, I set out to learn about the different jobs at the track. I started with the first job usually offered to newcomers in the racing business—the hotwalker.

A hotwalker at a racetrack does just what the name suggests: walks hot horses around by hand until they are cool. Anyone familiar with horses is aware of the problems that can develop from putting a hot, sweaty horse straight back into his stall. So after every race or exercise the horse is walked for forty-five minutes to an hour—until his skin is dry and he is breathing normally.

A good hotwalker knows his or her horses, and understands that a horse who is racing fit will cool out faster than one just in from the farm. A hotwalker must also know when to let the horse stop for a drink, how much to let him have, and when the cooler, a lightweight blanket put on the horse to prevent him from getting a chill, can be slipped back from the ears to the withers.

One of the lowest-paid workers in racing, hotwalkers usually earn between $80 and $100 a week. Many young people use it as a stepping-stone to higher-ranking track jobs, but others stay hotwalkers because they enjoy it.

I talked to one young hotwalker, Cynthia Marsh, who had been walking hots for eight months.

"I took this job," she explained as I accompanied her and

Hotwalker on the job

her charge around the shedrow, the covered walking area in front of the stalls, "because I've always loved animals, especially horses. I used to ride whenever I could when I was growing up in Minnesota. When I couldn't, I pretended that my bike—it was an old blue thing—was the fastest horse in the West."

Cynthia is a college graduate who came to New York straight out of school and took her first job with an advertising agency in Manhattan.

"I was never really happy there," she said. "Finally, after two years of listening to my complaints, a friend suggested that I apply for a job at the track. The idea seemed bizarre at first, but the more I thought about it, the more it appealed to me.

"Of course my parents weren't really pleased with my decision at first. You know, 'My daughter, the hotwalker,' but I like it here. It's a long day. I start around five-thirty in the morning and if the horses are running I might not be out of here until six or seven at night. There's no time for a social life outside the track. On the other hand, there is something really nice about being up at dawn. Everything looks so fresh and clean. And the horses," she said, pausing to run her hand over the soft muzzle of the horse she was walking, "these horses are the most beautiful animals in the world."

Cynthia lives close to the track and shares an apartment and living expenses with another girl who is an exercise rider. I asked Cynthia if she also wanted to ride.

"I probably would try to become an exercise rider, if I stayed," she answered. "But right now I'm not sure if I want to spend the rest of my life on the track and that's an easy thing to fall into. I've been thinking of maybe going to veterinary school. I guess what I'm really doing is trying to decide what to do with my life and being a hotwalker is a good way to earn some thinking time."

As Cynthia found out, however, you can never afford to let your attention wander too far while walking a thousand-pound, highly excitable animal.

"I had a two-year-old," she remembered, "and I should have known better because two-year-olds are not accustomed to the track like the older horses. Everything sets them off.

"Well, we were just coming around the corner of the shedrow and I was looking out the window at the rain when someone dropped a bucket. You'd think someone had shot a rifle the way the horse reacted. He just reared up, pulled the lead rope out of my hands, and took off. Luckily, he didn't get out of the barn, but he ran all over people and other horses and a couple of surprised stable cats before we caught him. On top of being pretty embarrassed, I had to start all over again with him. He was just as sweaty as if he'd raced around the track."

I asked her if she found walking hots hard work; you are on your feet most of the day.

"It's not really tiring once you get used to it," she said. "Except in bad weather. If it's freezing outside or raining hard, then the only exercise a horse might get that day is your walking him. If he's used to regular work and is penned up in the shedrow for a couple of days, he's going to be a handful. Also, the traffic in here will be fairly heavy because the exercise riders will be walking or trotting the horses around, too.

"Despite all of the obvious drawbacks to this work, it does have its rewards. For one thing, I enjoy the people I work with. You always hear stories about shady track characters, but I haven't run into many. Mostly, people are just concerned with the well-being of the horses, and I figure that can't be too bad.

"The horses, of course, are the main reason for staying. It's nice the way they depend on you. Even though they are big and strong, they are also fragile. And they have such different personalities—one might be hotheaded and willful, another one kind and easygoing. When they win, you feel like *you* just won. It's really like we're all working together for one goal."

I asked Cynthia if it is difficult to get a job as a hotwalker.

"It helps to know something about horses, naturally. Luck also has something to do with it—just being in the right place at the right time. I think if you want to work with racehorses and you don't give up, you can do it. One thing that's nice is that the stables aren't afraid of hiring women."

They aren't. In the Calumet Stable at Belmont, for example, half of the grooms, hotwalkers, and exercise riders are women. Many stables prefer to hire women because they feel women are more sympathetic toward the horses, and will tend to soothe a troublesome horse rather than whack him.

One track official, who asked not to be named ("or else I'll have the guys after me"), said that in his opinion the women were far superior to the men.

"They really care about the horses," he said, "and they're here because they want to be here, not because they're out of work and can't find anything better to do."

I left the barn just as Cynthia was turning the cooled-out horse over to a groom and picking up another one fresh from the track.

"So how are you doing this morning, Sam?" she asked.

("I call all the horses Sam, it's easier," she explained.)

The big filly blew through her nose and did a little stamping dance with her front feet in reply.

"Sure, sure," Cynthia said, as she took the lead shank and picked up the filly's walking stride.

Another woman, Carole Welker, who is now assistant secretary to the New York Thoroughbred Owners and Breeders Association, also started out at the track as a hotwalker. She was managing editor of a New York publishing house when she came to the Belmont backstretch with a friend on a visit. She liked what she saw and quit her job to walk hots. She worked for trainer John Rigione for about seven years, and progressed from hotwalker to assistant trainer before she quit her stable job to work full-time as secretary to the Association.

Her advice to young people who want a job working with racehorses is to see if there is a breeding farm nearby and go there to look for a job. If that isn't possible, she recommends going to one of the schools that offer horse-related courses. You can just show up at a racetrack as she and Cynthia Marsh did and hope to find a job, but, she said, an awful lot of luck is involved in that approach.

"If you get a job at a racehorse breeding or training farm," she said, "then you have the opportunity to go with the horses to the track. And it's entirely different on a farm. The horses here are all racing fit, and like any athlete in its prime, they're tense. But on a farm the horses are relaxed. They might not be that fit, and they themselves are young, so a young person *can* walk a horse. By the time you're sixteen or eighteen and ready to work at the track, you've had some valuable contact with racehorses."

2
Exercise Rider

Despite the many stories and articles written over the past few years about the growing role of women at the race-track, I was surprised the first time I went to watch the early morning workouts at Belmont. Easily a third of the riders were women.

Singly, in pairs, or in groups, the horses galloped by, nostrils flaring and mane and tail—and sometimes pigtails—flying.

Nicola Penn, twenty-seven, is an exercise rider for Sally Bailie, one of the foremost women trainers in the business. When I talked to Nickie about her work it was late morning and she was busy cleaning tack. The job of an exercise rider, it seems, is more than just galloping horses.

Nickie, who comes from Kentucky, was brought up around horses. She had ponies and horses of her own when she was young, and she showed hunters as a junior.

Nickie is tiny and extremely fragile-looking; she's not only short but also slim. It's hard to imagine that this pretty girl with a clean, open face and long blonde hair hanging in a single braid down her back makes her living guiding thousand-pound horses around the track.

I asked why she had turned to racehorses rather than pursuing a career as a show rider.

"Well, I never thought I was *that* good," she laughed, "and the field for a professional rider is so competitive. It's also expensive. It can cost as much to keep a show horse on the road as it does to train a racehorse. At least with these horses you have a chance to win some money back."

Nickie started working with racehorses as a hotwalker on a breeding farm in Kentucky. She got the job through her father, who was a friend of the owner. She would work in the mornings before going to school, and on weekends. Later, she started breaking yearlings.

"The way we would break a yearling," she said, "was to put a saddle on the horse while he was in his stall. Each day we would tighten up the girth a little more. We would also put the bridle on and let him get used to wearing them both in the security of his stall.

"After a while I would 'belly-up'—lie across the saddle. Someone else would be there with me to hold the horse and then lead him around with me lying on him. Some horses don't take to the idea right away, and I always had to be ready to make a quick dismount.

"It was a fantastic job for me. I rode them until they were ready to race. I got them started breezing."

Nickie explained that a breeze is faster than a gallop. In a gallop the horse is eased along with the rider standing up in the stirrups and maintaining a firm hold on the reins. In a breeze, the rider crouches low over the horse like a jockey in a race and asks the horse to show real speed.

She went on to say that some owners start training their horses for the track as early as the horse's first birthday, so the horses had "barely been on the ground" a year. But most

Exercise riders in an early morning gallop

trainers will wait until the following fall, when the horses are more mature. After a few weeks of being turned out in the summer, the horses are sent to a training center where they learn about breezing, starting gates, and the racetrack before they're shipped to the track to run for real.

Nickie worked at a number of breeding farms and training farms, breaking and training young horses, before she went to New York three years ago to work as an exercise rider.

I asked if she was ever apprehensive about galloping such high-strung horses. I had seen more than one horse take hold of the bit and gallop by me with the rider standing straight up in the stirrups, laying all his or her weight against the horse's mouth, but to no avail. And I had heard stories

of horses suddenly throwing a buck (while galloping at speeds up to forty miles an hour), sending the rider flying, or of horses jumping the guard rail and sending their rider through the air.

But Nickie just shrugged nonchalantly.

"Sometimes on a new horse I'm a little nervous," she said. "But once I've ridden a horse I'm not afraid of him. When you ride a horse for the first time, you don't know what he's going to do, or how he's been trained.

"Some horses don't know anything and that can get scary. Sometimes at the training track where I used to work, they'd ask me to ride a horse that was supposed to be completely trained. But then I'd get on him and he'd be dead green, he wouldn't even know how to trot, and I was supposed to have him ready to be breezed for prospective buyers in two weeks! That was rough.''

A typical day will find Nickie up between 4:30 and 5:00 A.M. in order to be at the track by 5:30 to start exercising. She might take a horse to the training track for a slow canter, usually with Sally Bailie riding alongside. Next, a green horse might go to the pony track, a small quarter-mile track, for a few laps around at a trot. And a horse that is being prepared for an upcoming race will be taken to the main track for a fast workout along the rail.

The exercise rider plays an important role in the preparation and training of the racehorse. To be effective the rider must have enough ability and control to get the required performance out of the horse, and carry out the trainer's instructions to the letter. Trainers bring their horses along according to a slow and carefully planned program. If an exercise rider deviates from that program, by allowing the horse to gallop too fast or for too long before it is ready, for example, the entire course of the horse's progress could be upset.

Nickie said that the most common way of getting a job galloping racehorses is to start out as a hotwalker, or possibly as a groom. Then, once you are familiar with the horses and trainers, and provided that you know how to ride, you can work your way up.

However, she did warn that the atmosphere at the track can be hard on a newcomer, and you're certainly not going to get rich as an exercise rider. You can expect somewhere around $150 a week as a full-time rider. Free-lance riders usually get $5 per horse, and a busy free-lancer can ride up to ten horses a morning, but this varies from day to day.

Unfortunately, some trainers will take advantage of a

"greenie." Nickie told me that when she was new to the business, she worked for a couple of trainers who had her doing more than the usual amount of hard work for less than the usual low pay. Check around to be sure you are working for a reputable trainer.

When asked what she saw herself doing ten years from now—working as a trainer?—Nickie frowned and said she was in the midst of thinking through a decision about her future.

"I love galloping horses," she said, her face lighting up. "Sometimes I can't believe I'm getting paid to do something I love, but after a while reality takes over and I have to think about where it's all leading. It's probably time that I left the track, but that's really a difficult decision for me to make.

"I only have one more year to get my degree in economics. What I would like to do is get that degree and then find a job outside the track, make a lot of money, and then buy and train my own racehorses. I could stay on here and work my way up the way Sally has, but that's really the hard way."

The following morning I found a crowd of racehorses and stable ponies building up at the entrance to the track, waiting for the harrowing to be finished. (At periodic intervals throughout the morning, as well as after each race, the track closes down while harrowing trucks go around smoothing and evening out the surface.)

I talked for a few minutes to an exercise rider who was standing away from the others.

"Watch out for this mare," she warned good-naturedly. "She kicks."

Physically the opposite of Nickie, Nancy Peters is large-boned and robust looking. Originally from Maryland, she has a friendly, outgoing personality.

"I grew up dreaming of becoming a famous jockey," she said, laughing. "But then I just got too big; I would never be able to make the weight. As it turned out it's just as well, because in a few months I'm going to apply for my trainer's license; well, assistant trainer, actually."

When she was younger, Nancy helped out grooming and exercising horses in a local stable that hired out horses, and when she was nineteen she got a job as a hotwalker at Pimlico in Maryland. A few months later she became an exercise rider and has been galloping horses ever since.

"I'm lucky to work for a trainer now who takes the time to show me what he's doing with the horses and why. It's been a great learning experience. The only way to become a trainer is to work for one. That way training techniques and decisions become second nature to you.

"You have to know so many things about the horses. Like when the horses are ready for the starting gate, when they're ready to be breezed, how fast you should ask them to go, when and if they need a break from training, and, of course, what to do with all the little emergencies that crop up every day.

"And something I didn't realize when I was getting started is that you also have to learn how to handle the owners."

Making a wry face, she explained, "The ones who know anything about the business are the easiest to work for. They'll let you take time with a horse to get him up to his full potential. But others, especially those who only have horses so they can gamble on them, just want results—and yesterday. Actually, that's the part of the business I'm least looking forward to."

Exercise rider (left) assisted by a pony rider

I asked if she regretted the fact that she couldn't be a jockey.

"No, not really," she said, shaking her head. "I've discovered that there's so much that goes into the training—before a horse ever gets to the starting gate—that it's always fascinating. And the job changes a little with each horse—each horse will teach you something else. I'm sure training is something I'll never get tired of."

The entrance gate opened again, and the horses started filing through.

"See you," she called cheerfully as she guided the mare onto the track. I watched as she gathered up the reins and, on the outside, going against traffic, moved up to a posting trot. In a few minutes she was back, galloping close to the rail, around the bend and out of sight.

Sometimes a trainer wants a horse exercised, but not ridden. That is the job of the pony riders. They lead the racehorses around the track while riding another horse. (Incidentally, a "pony" at the racetrack refers to any horse that is not a racehorse. It doesn't mean the small horses you usually associate with the word pony.)

Some of the larger stables at Belmont have their own ponies and pony riders. Others use the services of a friendly young man named Gary who operates a pony barn and employs several riders. He has a regular clientele of trainers who use him on a daily basis to pony one or more of their horses.

Some of the riders who work for Gary in the morning ponying horses also work at the races in the afternoon leading the thoroughbreds from the walking ring onto the track and up to the starting gate. If you have been to a

Angel Cordero escorted by a pony rider

racetrack or watched races on TV, you have probably seen them leading the racehorses onto the track and then trotting and cantering alongside as the thoroughbreds warm up for the race.

There are other riders out there on the track too. They are called outriders. Usually one outrider leads the horses to the starting gate while another brings up the rear. During the morning workouts outriders are stationed at strategic posts on the track.

Gary, who is also an outrider, describes the job as a combination of babysitter and lifeguard. It is up to them to catch runaways and loose horses. Sometimes a horse will get away from a pony rider. Or a horse and rider will part company. Other times a horse is too strong for the jockey or exercise rider and must be brought under control by the outrider.

"Five days a week you won't do anything," said Gary. "Then on the sixth you're picking up riders and horses all morning."

The morning I met him he was the outrider on duty at the pony track. The next morning, I took him up on his offer to get a firsthand look at the work of a pony rider. I rode one of his ponies and accompanied him on his rounds of picking up horses and taking them to the track for a workout. Gary was training a new pony he had just bought, and he had a rambunctious young filly in tow.

"The key to riding a pony," he explained as we did a slow gallop up the backstretch, "is to keep him straight. Most horses don't like the sensation of having a strange horse bump up against them. Some horses will veer away from the horse being led, or worse, try to kick it."

Gary watched the ears of the horse he was riding for any signs of bad temper. If the horse pinned them back flat against his head it might mean he was getting ready to kick or bite. But his new pony had a nice disposition and remained calm even when the filly playfully tried to take a bite out of his neck.

Gary explained that outriders are employed by the state racing association and are usually old-timers at the track who get the job through a recommendation. It is much easier to become a pony rider; in fact, Gary was currently looking for riders to work for him.

"If you can ride well and really handle a horse," he said, "you can always find a job at the track."

3
Jockey

Anyone who thinks that a jockey, even a top rider like Steve Cauthen or Willie Shoemaker, is someone who sits on a horse while the horse does all the running is in for a big surprise. The fact is that a good jockey must be a top athlete—intelligent, agile, strong, disciplined, *and* courageous. You cannot be timid and be a jockey, for every time the starting gate bangs open you run the risk of a bone-crushing disaster. When you're racing close together in packs of ten or more at top speeds of over forty miles an hour, there is no time to swerve or pull up to avoid an accident. If a horse takes a misstep or breaks a leg and goes down, chances are it will turn into a pileup with the jockeys flipped under falling horses or flying hooves. Wrecks are a hazard of the job and nearly every jockey has the broken bones and scars to prove it. Mary Bacon, one of the top women riders, has suffered a crushed pelvis, a punctured lung, a fractured skull, and three blood clots near the brain. She has broken her back in two places, her collarbone, three ribs, and bones in both feet and hands. The only protection against such accidents is a skull helmet worn inside the cap.

To make it to the top, a rider also needs tremendous skill,

Cordero and Cauthen are fourth and fifth from the right as they break from the gate.

split-second timing and reflexes, and an ability to "read" the faintest messages transmitted by the horse during the race.

Each horse is different and requires a slight adjustment in riding style. For example, once in stride, Secretariat liked a snugly drawn bit that would slow down most horses, and Forego would sulk if he was hit. His jockey would brandish the whip near the horse's right eye when he wanted more speed. Even more difficult are the horses who enjoy taking the lead early in a race, but who then think it is over and slow down or quit to finish back in the pack. The jockey almost has to trick them into winning—timing the surge to the lead to coincide with the finish line.

A jockey has to be savvy enough not to allow himself to

30

be boxed in by slower horses and nervy enough to turn a slight opening into a hole in which to drive his horse through. The best jockeys also have what is referred to as a "clock in the head." They can calculate to within a fraction of a second the speed at which they are traveling. In a business where winning is often measured by a whisper of the timer, this "clock in the head" is invaluable.

The first prerequisite of the job, however, is size. A jockey must be small. Robyn Smith, who carries her 102 pounds on a 5′ 7″ frame, is unusually tall for a jockey. With her angular features and height, she looks like a model. The average weight of a jockey is 110 pounds. Ironically, although many riders go to extremes to keep their weight down—constant dieting, vomiting after meals, or sweating off pounds in a steam room—it is a disadvantage to be too light. Often trainers or owners are prejudiced against "dead" weight, which refers to lead-weighted saddlepads. They will take a heavier rider over a featherweight who must use a weighted pad to meet the weight required in the race. When veteran rider Willie Shoemaker, 4′ 11″ and only 94 pounds, first started racing, he had to prove that dead weight when used by a rider with perfect balance is just as good, if not better, than live weight. He has since become famous for a quiet, unobtrusive style of riding. He coaxes a horse to the wire.

Aspiring jockeys, like almost everyone else in the racing business, must start at the bottom, mucking out stalls, soaping leather halters, saddles, and bridles, and walking hot horses. Robyn Smith, who didn't get on a horse until she was twenty, drove sixty miles every day to scrub saddles and clean horses when she was trying to break into the business.

The next step is exercising horses. You might spend anywhere from one to three years galloping horses under the instruction of a trainer before you are ready to race as an apprentice. To be granted an apprentice license, you must be at least sixteen and under a written contract to an owner or trainer. If you are underage, you must also have the permission of your parents to race.

Apprentice riders are given a weight allowance to help offset their inexperience and to give them a chance against the veteran riders. A beginning rider is given a ten-pound weight allowance, which means that he or she rides ten pounds lighter than the others in the race. This allowance is indicated by three asterisks after the rider's name in the entries. These asterisks are commonly referred to as "bugs" and the apprentice rider is called a bug boy (or girl). After the apprentice has accumulated five wins, the weight allowance is reduced to seven pounds and two bugs. After thirty-five wins, the rider is given a five-pound, one-bug allowance which remains until a year has elapsed, when he or she becomes a journeyman rider. In major stakes races, however, the weight allowance does not apply.

Throughout this training period apprentice riders follow a rigorous routine to keep fit and to sharpen their racing skills. They begin each day by galloping horses from dawn until about ten o'clock in the morning. After a short break for a meal and possibly a rest, they are back on the track. They must report to the Jockey Room an hour before post time (the first race of the day) and remain there until they have completed their races for the day.

One of the most important people in a jockey's life is his or her agent. It is up to the agent to contact the owners and trainers and book the best possible horses for the jockey.

The agent receives a percentage of the money earned, and can only work for one journeyman rider at a time. The jockey is paid a flat fee for each race and ten percent of the purse won. The possible earnings are high, but out of the 1,500 or so jockeys racing in this country, only a handful have reached economic and professional independence. For every rider taking his or her choice of mounts at Belmont or Santa Anita, there are dozens who never break out of the small town tracks.

One of the most famous young apprentice riders to break into the big time is Steve Cauthen. When he graduated from the small tracks of Ohio and Kentucky to the prestigious New York raceways, he did so by breaking records that had stood for twenty-five years. In a remarkably short time he accumulated the most wins in one day, the most wins in a row, and the most wins in a race meeting. Detractors said his astonishing performance was due to his bug boy status, but apprentice riders come and go every racing season without approaching a fraction of what he accomplished. After his first year of racing, Cauthen was proclaimed the most successful jockey in the world for winning purses in excess of six million dollars. The following year, in 1978, he guided the talented colt Affirmed in a series of brilliant rides to win the Kentucky Derby, the Preakness, and the Belmont, becoming the youngest jockey to ride a horse to a sweep of racing's coveted Triple Crown.

After a run of bad luck that would have daunted a veteran rider—an accident that put him out of action for over a month, a string of losing horses, and a falling out with his agent—Cauthen quietly predicted he would soon ride out his slump. He then moved to England and proved his versatility and skill as a race rider by adapting to the English style of riding and winning on his first day out. American racetracks, with their smooth ovals and uniform surfaces, are as tame as merry-go-rounds when compared to the uneven, hilly, and often treacherous terrain of the English courses. To date only two American riders, Shoemaker and Cauthen, have been able to compete successfully on them.

"I always wanted to be just one thing," says Steve, "to be a race rider." Brought up with horses, he had the best possible background for an aspiring jockey. His mother and two uncles are racehorse trainers and his father is a blacksmith. He was on his first pony when he was two years old and was galloping thoroughbreds across fields by five. So it was no surprise to the Cauthen family when Steve announced that he wanted to become a jockey. He and his father embarked on a strenuous training program. They borrowed race films from a nearby track and spent hours poring over them, dissecting the strengths and weaknesses of the jockeys. Cauthen saw that the race could be lost before it even began by a poor break from the starting gate. He watched as riders pumped with their bodies and flailed their arms in an effort to get speed from the horse, and he decided that they were only disrupting the horse's balance. Cauthen developed a style of riding similar to Shoemaker's. He sits still and low behind the neck of the horse—to decrease wind resistance and hinder the horse as little as possible.

Cauthen also spent hours sitting on a bale of hay with a pair of reins tacked in front of him practicing holding the reins and using the whip. By the time he was finished, he could switch the whip from hand to hand without dropping the reins, and hit to within an eighth of an inch of where he wanted to hit. When it finally came time to start exercising horses, he galloped every horse that came his way, never turning down a rogue or a difficult horse. And he listened. If a trainer wanted a certain ride or had a piece of advice, Cauthen only had to be told once.

When he turned sixteen and rode in his first race as an apprentice, Cauthen had months of valuable experience behind him, riding, watching, and learning. But there was something more. Trainers talked of his hands, of his way with horses. From the start, his riding was marked by an indescribable brand of communication between himself and his horses. He seemed to instill confidence and courage into

The final turn toward the wire

the horses he rode, as over and over they showed speed and boldness for him that they had not displayed before.

Cauthen had a distinct advantage in growing up in a horse-oriented environment. Angel Cordero, the popular and winning rider from Puerto Rico, was also a "barn rat." His father exercised horses for a living and Cordero grew up in a stable handling horses. Many other jockeys do not begin to ride, however, until a late-developing interest or their special size and weight bring them to the track. Jeffrey Fell, a talented young rider from Canada, didn't get on a horse until he was sixteen. Fell played center for a hockey team until he decided that, as an 85-pounder, the sport was demolishing him. He rode in his first race when he was seventeen and is now riding against the best—and winning—at the top United States tracks. Completely dedicated to his profession, Fell gets up at five to exercise horses, and arrives in the Jockey Room three hours early to study films from the previous day's racing.

Becoming a top jockey requires long hours of hard work and driving determination. Although the possible rewards are great, the odds against succeeding are high. Many riders flash briefly as long as they have the weight allowance, but fade when they lose their bug status. Others succumb to the easy life that sudden wealth can bring and fall out of training. Anyone thinking of becoming a race rider must be prepared to face the rougher aspects of the job—the constant physical danger, the difficulty in keeping weight down and strength up, and the often demoralizing mercurial aspects of racing glory. As one trainer told me, "If you haven't won a race in the past fifteen minutes, they forget who you are."

Jockeys fight against a lot of difficulties, and women

jockeys have the added burden of proving their worth in this aggressive, male-oriented profession. It wasn't until the late 1960s that women were licensed to race. Kathy Kusner, an Olympic jumping rider, was the first to sue for and win the right to be a jockey. Before she got the chance, however, she hurt her leg in a fall in a horse show and was out of action for several months. Penny Ann Early then tried four times to get booked at Churchill Downs but was met with stiff boycotts. Finally, on February 7, 1969, Diane Crump rode at Hialeah in Florida. She was the first woman jockey to appear at a major track.

Since that time women have been riding, and winning, at major tracks across the country. But it is still very much a man's business. Owners and trainers are wary of hiring female jockeys. The successful women riders clear in excess of $65,000 a year, however, and as more women prove themselves winners, the prejudices against them will inevitably fade. Robyn Smith refutes the claim of some trainers that women aren't strong enough to handle a racehorse. "You need some strength to race a horse," she says, "but you don't manhandle it. You need a certain rapport with the animal." As one female exercise rider said to me, "I *ride* the horse, I don't carry it."

4

Racehorse Trainer

When I first met Sally Bailie she was up on a stable pony preparing to ride out with Nickie Penn, her full-time exercise rider. She was instructing Nickie to walk the filly she was on around the paths of the backstretch. Lethargic and let down, the filly wasn't fit enough for anything more strenuous.

Sally mentioned to me that the filly had had an ankle problem and they were trying to get her back into racing shape.

"Which one is swollen?" I asked, casting a suspicious eye on the right front.

"All of them," answered Sally dryly.

Actually, they had all looked fine to me.

Later that morning, when all the horses had had their exercise and things were beginning to quiet down in the barn, Sally settled down in the tack room with me to talk about the business.

A strong and capable-looking woman in her forties with a decidedly British accent, Sally has a wry sense of humor and a no-nonsense, look-you-dead-in-the-eye gaze. I asked Sally how she had gotten her start to become one of the more prominent women trainers in horse racing.

"I grew up on a farm in England, and we had cows and chickens, and we had to do everything to take care of them," she answered.

"I was more interested in the horses than I was in the other animals. But the horses had to be secondary because there wasn't any money in them. The farm work had to be done first, such as milking the cows and the rest. After my mother died, we had to sell the farm, and the only things I knew how to do were drive a tractor, milk a cow, and ride a horse.

"I decided that riding horses was better than milking

Sally Bailie (left) escorting Nickie Penn through the Belmont backstretch

cows—I always liked driving tractors, but that's not the point—so I worked private jobs training steeplechase jumpers.

"I had trained steeplechase jumpers myself when we had our own farm. I used to train and ride them. They didn't belong to me; I was doing this for other farmers, and I was lucky enough to win quite a few races. So I didn't have much problem getting a job when we sold the farm."

In 1965 Sally Bailie came over to the United States, but since she didn't know how long she was going to stay, she said she "putted around for a year and had jobs doing different things."

She worked with steeplechasers for a while, and then worked at a couple of flat—non-jumping—stables. She was an assistant trainer for four and a half years. In 1970 she got her trainer's license, built up a clientele, and started her own business.

Although Sally had come to the States with a good background with steeplechase horses, most of her work here has been with flat horses. She explained the similarities and the differences in training the two kinds.

"The training is a little bit different for two reasons. One, you've got to teach steeplechasers to jump. The other is that steeplechase horses go three miles, and these animals"—she pointed to the stalls across the aisle—"go for six furlongs. It's a whole different concept in training. You train these horses short and sharp, and steeplechasers for the long distance.

"The basic care though—the bandages, taking care of the legs—is obviously the same. Except the steeplechasers you'll get are generally older and they develop different kinds of problems from a young horse. The young horse is still growing and the old horse's bones have settled. Bone tendons are the main thing with steeplechasers. These young horses have problems with ankles and knees and so forth."

A blacksmith popped his head in the door and told Sally he was ready to do her horse.

"Good," she said, going off to show him the horse. "Could you just cut his heel out a tiny bit?"

When she came back I asked if she had found it difficult being a woman in what traditionally has been considered a man's business.

"In a way yes and in a way no," she answered. "I think that when I started people thought it was a little strange because there were only two other women trainers.

"I fell back on the fact that I was a woman anytime anybody gave me a hard time," she laughed. "For example, if I had difficulty getting stalls. But in actual fact, it wasn't because I was a woman, but because I had a bunch of cheap horses."

Sometimes Sally thinks being a woman is a good lever, and in a business as tough and competitive as horse racing, you need all the levers you can get.

Sally lamented that for the moment her barn of nine horses consisted mainly of two-year-olds.

"Two-year-olds are great," she said. "But they have so many problems. They're just like kids growing up. Kids get chicken pox and measles, and the young horses get fevers and bucked shins. Every time you think you've got them half there, something else goes wrong. But they're interesting because you can see them change. They come off the farm fat and sleepy-eyed, and then you see them get fit and strong and ready to race."

Sally would like to have her own horses to train, but at this point she cannot afford the initial capital investment. All the horses under her care belong to other people. She receives a flat fee for training, and then gets a percentage of the purses.

"The flat fee doesn't cover the cost of keeping all these bums walking around here," she chided affectionately at two of her stablehands. Nickie, preparing leg wraps, looked

Trainer with young horse on the Belmont pony track

up and smiled, and Jamie, her groom, just laughed to himself.

"We just about cover costs," she went on. "You're always looking for the winners because that's the only way you can make it."

Just then Jeff Minton, a representative of the New York Thoroughbred Owners and Breeders Association, stopped in to talk with Sally.

"How's your big horse going to do?" he asked.

"I don't know. I'll let you know a little later," Sally replied.

The horse in question was Poison Ivory, a New York bred three-year-old colt. Up to this point in the current Belmont race meeting, Sally hadn't been able to get a horse to the post. She had had numerous problems with her good horses; one was sent home and another was claimed from her in a claim race. (In a claim race the horses are entered at a stated price and may be purchased by any other owner of a starter in the race.)

Steve Cauthen, who had had his choice of either the ranked favorite of the day or Poison Ivory, had decided to ride Ivory. A good omen, I thought, but Sally is not the type to put much faith in omens.

Minton glanced over at Jamie, who looked like he was mixing a bucket of cement.

"You can tell when we're getting ready to run," said Sally. "Jamie is up to his elbows in poultice every morning. If there's no medication to be done, you know you're in trouble. It's the total reversal of what it should be."

Jeff and Sally discussed distances and dirt tracks versus grass, and then he left, wishing her luck.

Sally then explained to me that the difference between a

dirt and grass track can have a tremendous effect on the outcome of a race.

"Some horses will run better on grass than they do on dirt," she said. "Most of them run pretty well on either. I know someone who had a horse, a $25,000 claimer, who couldn't get out of his own way on the dirt, and they put him on the grass and he took off. He won stakes. I mean major stakes, not itty-bitty little stakes.

"On the other hand, I had a filly a couple of years ago that was dynamite on the dirt. I tried her out on the grass one day because she liked to run long distances, and most grass races are a distance, and my God, I think she was beaten by something like fifty-five lengths. It was embarrassing. She just hated the grass and wouldn't go.

"That kind of thing does happen. A lot of times you'll have a horse you know can run, but he's not winning. So you'll try him short, you'll try him long—you'll give him every shot you can."

Another way of giving her horses every shot she can is by running a smoothly functioning stable. It would be a temptation, when working on a tight budget, to cut corners, but as Sally said, "You can't cut corners and win races."

She has seven people working for her, including grooms, exercise riders, and hotwalkers, all of whom she thinks of as a necessity, not a luxury. She feels that if you cut your help down, the work doesn't get done as well as it should.

"The overhead of having extra help pays off in the end when you get to running them because you know you've done the best you can with the horse. When you have a racehorse, everything has got to be done right."

On a typical day, Sally is up at 4:30 A.M. and is at the barn by 5:15. Neal, her free-lance exercise rider, who takes the horses that are too strong for Nickie, is on his first horse at 5:30. Sally will tack up a stable pony to ride over to the track to watch her horses being exercised. She then oversees all the horses being bandaged and she examines their legs the following morning before they go out again.

Sometime around midmorning when the bulk of the work has been done, there is a break for breakfast, and hopefully there is time to lie down for half an hour before post time at 1:30.

Sally stops by the barn before the race to make sure everybody is organized—that the horse has bandages if he needs them, and that her people are ready to go over with him when he's called. Then she'll go over to the paddock, talk with the jockey and the owner, meet her people, and saddle up the horse.

After the races, when she's certain that everything has been attended to at the barn, she goes home for a light dinner and maybe an hour or two of TV. The day usually ends with bed at nine o'clock.

Feeling guilty that the interview was probably cutting into her rest time, I asked Sally one final question: Did she have any words of advice to a young person who wants to be a trainer?

"Stay away!" she answered in mock horror. "Seriously, you have to have a basic upbringing with horses before you're going to go anywhere.

"For example, one trainer I know started out in a hack stable in Brooklyn somewhere. He was there every morning mucking out stalls and taking care of all the horses and he learned from them, but he started out when he was a kid.

"You'll find that most of your good trainers and most of the people who know horses best have been with them since they were little. They were all brought up in the barn. The people who were brought up with horses have got much more of an advantage."

Later in the day, I waited anxiously for the third race to begin. Poison Ivory, with Cauthen up, took the lead early and led the pack of nine to the finish. He won it handily. Sally, changed from her work pants to a dress and with her long hair flowing loose, looking pleased and very much a winner herself, went to meet her horse and jockey in the winner's circle.

Cauthen on Poison Ivory

5
Veterinarian

Jimmy Belden, a veterinarian at Belmont racetrack, can be found in the early morning hours covering the backstretch with a small army of assistants. The life of a racetrack veterinarian is hectic at best, but Jimmy moves from stable to stable and horse to horse with quiet efficiency. A big man, he is surprisingly soft-spoken. You almost have to strain to catch his words.

On the morning I talked with him there was another veterinarian with him who wanted to make a career change from small animal practice to horses. Also there was a young woman, Judy, who was a veterinary student assisting him for the summer, along with a couple other young people serving as assistants. They weren't sure yet that they wanted to be vets, and this was a good way to find out.

When I met Dr. Belden he was halfway underneath a horse he was preparing for gelding. After he administered a local anesthetic, he straightened up and began to talk about his work. He told me he had always wanted to be a veterinarian.

"It's a great mixture of science and art. There's just enough science in the medicine to satisfy your scientific

Judy giving intravenous feeding

curiosity, and there's just enough art in the application of the science to make you feel a little bit like an artist and satisfy you that way. It's the kind of thing you can stay occupied with on a full-time basis, and you can support a family well and be happy about what you're doing."

While waiting for the anesthetic to work, he supervised as Judy administered an intravenous feeding of a vitamin supplement to another horse. He then moved down the aisle to perform the operation. Feeling a bit squeamish, I chose to stay and watch the intravenous feeding. In a short while, he called to me that it was safe for me to look, and I walked down the aisle to find the colt contentedly munching some hay. Aside from a few splatters of blood on Dr. Belden's pants, there was not much evidence of surgery.

I asked him how he had ended up working with horses.

"I just care more about horses," he answered. "I can relate better to horses, I guess, than any other class of animal or livestock."

Talking about the different areas of veterinary medicine, he said that the small animal practitioners on the average probably do better financially, largely because of the structure of the business. For example, they can build hospitals and build up an investment.

"The only equity we have is what we have in our inventory, our truck and any other special equipment we might have. So we really don't have anything to sell such as a location, hospital, or something of that nature. If you ever leave practice, you just leave practice."

Dr. Belden continued talking as we moved to another stable. A trainer was concerned about one of his horses that had developed a runny nose. Dr. Belden looked at the horse, decided what medication was necessary, and passed his instructions on to Judy, who noted it in her book.

"Most of us," he said, "have not found it economically feasible to associate in groups; consequently, in most instances we work seven days a week. Vacations are catch as catch can.

"Horses, unfortunately, particularly racehorses, have a tendency to fall prey to illnesses at all times of the day or night. They are, of course, extremely valuable, and even more than valuable, they're extremely fragile.

"These horses, because of their breeding or the intensity of their breeding, respond poorly to stresses, particularly fevers and infections. So that in the case of a bad infection and high fever an hour can make the difference between life and death. There are a lot of things that are of a very immediate nature and you find yourself being on call twenty-four hours a day."

Dr. Belden, gentle and affectionate with his patients, although firm when he has to be, stopped to scratch the head of a big chestnut that was thrust out as he walked by the stall.

He continued thoughtfully, "So basically the only drawbacks to large animal practice are the hours, the consistency of responsibility, and the fact that when you're all through practicing, in most instances you really have no facility to sell. But, on the other hand, you are your own boss for the most part, and you're not tied down by a facility that at least initially is going to cost several thousand dollars."

Dr. Belden is enthusiastic about racetrack practice for equine veterinarians. Even though his responsibilities seem to leave him with little or no time for himself, he enjoys the daily contact with his patients.

"Veterinary practice at the racetrack is for sure *the* most intense of any of the veterinary fields. Rarely does a day go by that you don't see your patient, stop to look at him, or treat him. Very rarely does a day go by that you don't see *all* of your patients. So you become close to them; you feel their successes and you feel their failures and their problems. And if you can help them overcome their problems and make a success of their lives, then you feel that you've been a success yourself."

Affirmed, the 1978 Triple Crown winner and one of Dr.

Belden's more successful patients, sticks his head out of his stall and nudges Dr. Belden's back for a rub. We laugh, and of course Affirmed gets what he wants. Standing in his box with just a halter, Affirmed looks something like a movie star caught at home without makeup.

"You're a good boy," Dr. Belden says as he scratches the horse's ear. "You know that, don't you?"

We continued on our rounds of the stables. Someone was always waiting for Dr. Belden—to show him a horse that had developed a problem, or to report on a patient's progress.

I know that horses have accidents and break down frequently on the track, and I asked him if he is involved in much surgery. He said he had been involved in it in the past, but has lost faith in the arguments for performing extensive surgery at the racetrack. He now limits himself to routine surgery and minor operations, such as tissue repair, castration, splints, and so forth, that can be handled with a local anesthetic.

Dr. Belden explained that rarely does a horse come back to the races after he has had serious surgery—only one out of ten returns who has had orthopedic surgery. And, he claims, since most of his patients can afford better medical care, he doesn't see the reasoning in performing a major operation under the moderately adverse conditions of the track.

Consequently, most major surgery is referred to a former classmate who is now head of the University of Pennsylvania's Equine Center at New Bolton. There is, of course, an emergency hospital available to the veterinarians at the track, but Dr. Belden said the facilities are semi-crude compared to those at New Bolton, so if an operation can be referred, it is. The owners want the best for their horses and appreciate Dr. Belden's honesty.

I asked Dr. Belden if anything ever bothered him about his work. Did he, for example, have to overcome an initial fear of cutting? He told me that since he grew up on a farm, where dead stock is a very real part of livestock, cutting and surgery never affected him. But euthanasia has always been hard for him to face.

"I always have to psych myself up," he said. "I have to rationalize and convince myself that it's absolutely necessary. I always feel a little depressed even though I know that the horse is relieved from suffering. And, of course, we don't consider animals to be possessed of an immortal soul. So all things considered, euthanasia is easily rationalized as a part of the practice. But I still get depressed, particularly if I've been close to the animal."

Dr. Belden went on to say that he must rationalize some aspects of his practice that he feels are not necessarily consistent with the horse's well-being. He was referring to some drugs, also given to human athletes, which are injected into arthritic joints. The horses are then given a rest and are raced again as soon as they are sound. This practice tends to be somewhat debilitating over a long period of time and the horses wind up with stiff joints.

"However," Dr. Belden explained, "I can satisfy myself by sitting down and thinking that these horses were born to be racehorses, they were bred to be racehorses, and if it weren't for horse racing they wouldn't be alive. They wouldn't be here. I wouldn't be here. None of this would be going on."

Dr. Belden will refuse to give these drugs, though, to the better horses. A horse that has won a significant number of

Jimmy Belden examining a horse in the shedrow

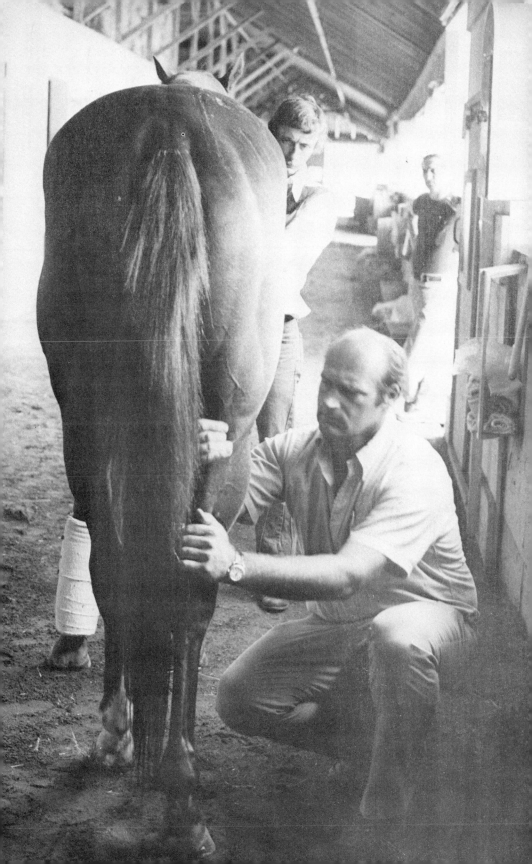

stakes has already solidified his position in the breeding industry. So if the horse is developing arthritis and can no longer run effectively, Dr. Belden won't take the chance of hurting him further.

Once we were on the subject of drugs, I brought up the controversy over the use of Butazolidin on racehorses. Some weeks earlier, a horse racing at Pimlico in Maryland broke a leg and the jockey, who was injured in the fall, blamed it on the drug the horse had been receiving.

Dr. Belden disagreed. "Where professionalism prevails, Butazolidin is not dangerous. Trainers and veterinarians pretty universally have a conscience, and you're certainly not going to run a horse with a broken leg.

"Bute doesn't hide major problems, it simply helps in the management of minor inflammatory conditions. Used as an adjunct, not as a substitute, to a lot of other things you do, it simply makes the horse more comfortable. People get into trouble with bute when they start using it as a substitute for good care. But I've never seen a horse in my life that had a serious, life-threatening defect that Butazolidin helped to the point that the horse would get by the examining veterinarian."

Every racetrack has an examining veterinarian who goes around in the morning and checks each horse scheduled to run that day. At Belmont the examining vet is Dr. Manuel Gilman.

First Dr. Gilman matches the horse to the chart he has on him. He identifies the horse by his markings and tattoo (under the upper lip). He then takes the horse's temperature and looks at his eyes. He superficially examines the legs and checks what he finds against the horse's prior record to see if there's been any change.

For example, if a tendon has always been thick and it's thick that day, he won't do anything, but if it's never been thick before, Dr. Gilman will scratch the horse.

Following Dr. Belden through the backstretch, I was amazed at the number of patients he looked at and treated in a working day. I felt somewhat like Alice following the Mad Hatter, although there is nothing mad or erratic in Dr. Belden's procedures. Quite the contrary, he is deliberate and efficient in his dealings with the horses, trainers, and grooms and with his assistants.

I asked if this had been a typical morning. To my surprise, he told me it had been slow.

"Sometimes," he said, "things get hectic. Some mornings three or four potential disasters occur at the same time. You don't know which way to turn next; you have to make yourself settle down and follow through.

"It might be that a horse has cut himself on the track or in the stall and is bleeding badly. That call comes in and you're on your way there, and the bleeper goes off and somebody else has a horse with a colic. So you're trying to decide which one to treat first. You rush over to stop the bleeding and then go to the horse with the colic, and the bleeper goes off again and a horse has broken a leg on the racetrack.

"So you dash off in the ambulance and bring him back to the barn, x-ray him, and make the decision: Can we save him or is it sufficiently bad so that the horse must be destroyed?

"These are the types of decisions you get involved in and you just have to cool your head and set up your own system of priorities. You have to decide what you can do on an immediate basis to sustain or stabilize one patient while you rush off to the next. Once you set up your routine, it's no big thing to follow through, but the pressure is there even though you know you're capable of handling it. It's sort of like being at the emergency room in a hospital right after a plane crash. Things are popping in too many places."

It was these sorts of emergencies plus the pressure of a too-big caseload that made Dr. Belden the victim of a heart attack in 1970. This happened while he was working at another New York track. He had a couple of other veterinarians working with him and the practice was, as he puts it, "a monster."

He turned the entire practice over to one of the vets who was working with him and moved to Belmont with the idea of developing a small, selective group of clients and trying to make it by himself on a smaller basis. Dr. Belden realized that, for him, working with associates was unsatisfactory.

"In order to make a practice effective," he said, "there has to be one way of doing things. Even though you might not like imposing your will, someone has to be boss. So anything that anybody did, I had to be on top of: public relations, assisting in diagnosis, assisting in treatment, and keeping track of everything—I was going crazy."

Dr. Belden now has nine major stables that he deals with, three of which he shares with another veterinarian. This constitutes a total caseload of 372 horses, 260 of which are his sole responsibility.

Once the bulk of the day's work was over, the crew stopped for a late barbeque lunch in back of Dr. Belden's office. As his assistants were busy getting the fire started and the food out, Dr. Belden offered his advice to aspiring veterinarians.

"Probably the most important thing to stress if you want to be a veterinarian," he said reflectively, "is not the hard

56

work. The hard work is easy, if you're used to working with animals.

"The most important thing to stress is to get exposure to the type of animals that are going to be your patients, and to do this preferably in a farm setting. That way you get to know what these animals' normal behavior patterns are, what their normal requirements to stay alive are—their routines, their feeding schedule.

It's so much easier to recognize problems if you are familiar with the animal's normal behavior, but you don't get much of that familiarity in college. So the first thing is to get plenty of animal experience."

Would he recommend the equine practice?

"If you are concerned about amassing a large amount of money," he warned, "then probably the large animal practice is not the ideal for you. But if you're interested in making a comfortable living and practicing your skills, and doing something that you can get your heart into, then I would recommend this."

6
Riding Instructor

When I arrived at Suburban Essex Riding Club in New Jersey to interview two riding instructors, I found them both working with students in the large indoor arena.

Sheila Curren had a student at the far end of the ring on a longe rein. Marsha Bancroft was helping another student adjust her stirrups and tighten the girth. The woman looked a little worried, but she settled down under Marsha's instruction. Soon both she and the horse were relaxed as they walked, trotted, and cantered the wall track.

Sheila was the first to finish. She unhitched the horse from the longe and had her rider execute a walk, trot, and halt on his own. The rider seemed excited and pleased—it was only his second lesson. Sheila seemed just as satisfied.

Once the arrangements for the next lesson were made, Sheila and I moved to an office with a view of the ring to talk about her career as a riding instructor. She told me that she had liked horses since she was very young.

"I pestered my parents until they let me take lessons," she said. "I was ten at the time, and I had lessons once or twice a week, just like most of the riders starting here. By the time I was thirteen, I had gone to some small, local shows and my parents decided to buy me a horse.

"We did fairly well together. He didn't look nice like a hunter should, and he didn't go quietly enough for equitation classes, so I showed in junior jumpers. When I was eighteen my horse was New Jersey AHSA (American Horse Shows Association) Junior Jumper champion and Garden State Junior Jumper reserve champion."

Sheila began teaching informally while she was still in high school. The manager of the stable where she boarded her horse asked her to help out when he was teaching group lessons. If there was a rider who was not able to follow the class, Sheila would ride next to that person and help him or her, freeing the instructor to take the group through more difficult routines.

"I would do that every once in a while as a favor," she said, "and I decided that I liked teaching. I liked being able to help."

Sheila's first "real" teaching job also originated as a favor. The stable sent several of its horses to summer camp during the slow summer months. When the manager suddenly had to find a replacement for his regular instructor at the camp, he sent Sheila.

"I loved it," she said. "The next year he sent his horses to a different camp and I went with them. The following year I did the same thing, and when I came back he had bought another stable that he wanted me to run for him."

Aside from working for a year in an office when that stable was sold, Sheila has been working with horses ever since.

She found that one of the drawbacks of instructing, however, was that she no longer had time for showing. The stable Sheila managed was a small one, and she and the other instructors had to do everything from feeding and grooming to cleaning tack. The only job they didn't do was muck out the stalls.

Although Sheila still rides every day, she no longer has her own horse.

"I sold him to a girl who was thirteen," said Sheila, "the same age I was when I bought him. She had him for ten years and he died at the age of twenty-five after having nineteen years with two people. So he had a pretty good life!"

Marsha Bancroft joined us after she finished her lesson. Her start in the business was similar to Sheila's. She grew up loving horses and riding whenever she could. Although she didn't own a horse when she was young, she taught riding at summer camp and later in college. Marsha was thoughtful as she explained how she started working with horses.

"I grew up in the 1950s," she said, "and it never occurred to me that I was supposed to have a career. I was supposed to get married and have children and that's what I did. I probably never would have gotten involved with horses if we hadn't moved next door to a riding stable.

"I took some lessons and told the owner that if he needed help I would like to work for him. He called when there was an opening, and that's how it started. When my children were small they would go to the house across the street or come to the stable. It was very convenient living next door!"

Marsha has owned or shared seven horses since she started working. But, like Sheila, she has always found that time is a problem—some days are just too hectic to ride.

A typical working day varies from stable to stable. In the smaller stables the instructors usually do more than just teach. They may do the feeding, grooming, tacking up,

Marsha Bancroft helping student adjust stirrups

administering of medication, and mucking out stalls as well. Since it's often in the smaller stables that you get your first job, you must be willing to work from the bottom up.

"It involves innumerable hours," Sheila warned. "If you can't get the job done in a reasonable amount of time, you can't just walk away and leave, because the horses have to have the attention. They can't feed themselves or clean their own stalls. Before I came here, I worked seven days a week. Also, vacations are difficult when you're running a stable. Replacements are hard to find. It must be somebody reliable who knows the animals."

At the larger, commercial stables such as Suburban Essex, which comfortably houses over 120 horses, it is more a strictly teaching situation. On occasion Sheila and Marsha school a horse or take care of a sick animal, but basically their job is instructing. Unlike the instructors at smaller stables where the hours can be unpredictable, Sheila and Marsha work a regular schedule—nine-to-six on the day shifts, and one-to-ten on the evening shifts.

Both Sheila and Marsha love their work, but are quick to point out that it's not without its hardships.

"You can't sit down and teach riding," Marsha told me. "You're on your feet most of the day. Another major factor in teaching is that there is a certain amount of risk involved in riding a horse. You constantly have to be aware of the safety of the rider and the unpredictability of the horse. Children present their own set of problems. Often they are too small to be strong enough to control the horse.

"There is a lot of brain work involved in teaching riding. When you're instructing beginners, you are dealing with very timid people and you have to work hard to build up their confidence. You can't have them doing the same thing over and over again or you will bore them, so you have to put thought into your lessons. It looks easier than it is."

They explained that in stables that don't have an indoor ring, weather is also a factor.

"One winter we were teaching outside in five degrees," Marsha remembered. "We put a big drum in the middle of the field and built a fire in it to keep warm. Every morning we had to make a manure track in the ring for the horses to work on, otherwise they would have been skidding on the snow and ice."

Marsha pointed out another, more practical consideration when thinking about a career as a riding instructor, and that is the money involved.

"It's not one of the higher-paying jobs," she said. "You have to like what you're doing because you're not going to get rich doing it."

Some instructors, notably those involved with the show circuit, do command top fees. But, as Sheila explained, "We're not the stars; we provide for the stars. There is, of course, a greater need for people like us. Out of the thousands of people who ride, only a handful are going to go to Madison Square Garden. In terms of people going into a career with horses, unless they have had tremendous experience in the show world themselves, they will start low and take a long time to get to the top."

When asked what advice they had for a young person who wanted a career as a riding instructor, both said to get as much experience as possible with horses. They feel that the best thing a potential instructor can do is ride, and take lessons.

"Do as much riding with supervision as you can," Sheila advised. "Try to locate a stable whose primary function is instruction, rather than a hack stable where they just rent horses."

Marsha agrees. "Pick a reputable teaching stable and make yourself available to help in any capacity—grooming, cleaning stalls, whatever. If you own a horse, try to do some showing, even if it is only on a local level. Or try to get involved with somebody who has a horse and will let you show it with them, or for them. Ideally, after that I would say go to a college offering a horse-related degree or get an instructor's certificate from a good riding school."

More and more schools around the country are offering horse-related courses and degrees. However, as Sheila cautioned, a degree does not guarantee a job, and you should pick the school carefully.

"Unfortunately, not all of these places have the greatest reputation," she said. "They will take people without much riding experience and try to make teachers out of them. We've had some apply for jobs here full of theory. But theory doesn't always work because the horse hasn't read that book. It's not that these people can't ride, but that they haven't got practical stable experience. The person who goes into a school after having spent four or five years riding regularly, however, is going to make a good instructor and will also have a greater earning potential."

Another way to get into the business is to establish yourself on the show circuit. Many people who have been successful as show riders move into the teaching end of the business. Unfortunately, this route is not available to most people because of the time and expense involved.

I asked Sheila and Marsha, who have both been teaching now for several years, their plans for the future.

"I've thought of becoming a full-time stable manager, but

I don't have the personality for it," said Sheila. "I can do the work, but I'm not that good at dishing it out for other people and then checking up on them to see that they've done it. I would end up doing it myself, so I am better off having someone else tell me what to do unless it would be such a small operation that I could do it all myself."

Marsha feels the same way: "I wouldn't want to be a manager or an owner. This job is very gratifying. At the level we teach, beginners through intermediate, we see tremendous improvements in our students. We also see the great amount of pleasure that they're getting and that's rewarding. Both of us have a number of people who will only work with us, which is satisfying."

"I like to be able to instruct riders to the point where they are able to go beyond me," adds Sheila. "That's just as much fun for me as teaching the ones who are competing."

A large crash focused our attention on the ring. A horse had just deposited his rider into a jump. Nothing was injured but the rider's pride, and the horse was now assuming a nonchalant air.

The interruption brought us back to the present. Sheila looked at her watch and realized that they both had lessons about to begin. Getting ready to go back to the ring, she paused and summed up: "To answer your question, I love my work." Marsha agreed. "I don't think I would be happy doing anything else."

7
Trainer

Jimmy Williams, one of the leading trainers in the country today, operates a sprawling horse farm in southern California. His Flintridge Riding Club, a thirty-nine-acre spread picturesquely set in the hills above Pasadena, regularly produces top young riders and horses in the world of hunters and jumpers. His students have included Mary Mairs Chapot, a former U.S. Equestrian Team rider, and Robert Ridland, a current Team member. Francis Steinwedell, who won the Maclay trophy at Madison Square Garden in 1977, also trained with Williams.

A handsome man of sixty-one, his tanned face accented by silver-white hair, Jimmy Williams is charmingly unaffected. One raw, chilly morning—rare for that part of California—we sat in front of a crackling fire in his living room as he talked about his life working with horses. As with so many people in the horse business, Jimmy was born into it.

"I never knew anything else," he told me, "because on my mother's side and on my father's side, they were all horse people. My dad was a horse dealer, and his brother had racehorses. My mother's family also had racehorses."

As Jimmy says, he could "ride the tail off a horse" by the time he was eight or nine, and when he was twelve he was racing "steel-dust" horses—short distance horses—at the bush tracks. For a long time he was the leading short-horse jockey in the state.

Jimmy also rode horses for his father at the auctions on 25th Street in Los Angeles—as many as 100 to 150 horses a day—for ten dollars a day and fifty cents per horse. He rode every style: saddle seat, hunt seat, and Western. Dave Williams, Jimmy's father, who was one of the top horsemen in California, taught Jimmy how to train horses. Jimmy began his teaching career by showing people how to ride the horses they had bought from his father.

One day, while Jimmy was riding at the auction, he learned about a tryout run by a scout from MGM, who was looking for a stunt man for movie star Tyrone Power.

"I was a bit conceited," Jimmy remembers grinning, "because I had won a lot of races and a lot of stock horse classes. I just *knew* they were going to pick me. Anyhow, I went and there must have been twenty-five or thirty people trying out.

"My dad furnished the studios with all different kinds of horses, and he had sold MGM a horse for the Cisco Kid. A beautiful black horse that I had trained. He was the horse everybody was supposed to ride and try out!

"I knew one of the wranglers and I told him I had broke the horse. But I was way down the line. They had already had about five or six try out and the horse was throwing his head and fighting them all. It was terrible.

"Finally, the wrangler pointed me out to the assistant director, who came over and introduced me to the director. I got on this horse and clucked to him and put my legs on

Jimmy Williams competing in a Hunter class

him and he got 'bridled up.' I showed off in front of the camera and then I stepped off him like a cowboy, putting the reins over the horn, and he turned and faced me, blowing through his nose like a circus horse.

"That was it. They just excused everybody else and that's how I started doubling for Tyrone Power."

Jimmy continued training horses and competing in shows while working free-lance with the studios. Over the years he stunted in many films, including several with Power—*Marie Antoinette, The Mark of Zorro,* and *Suez* to name a few—but he said he found the work boring and preferred his horse business.

Even today, after countless shows and horses, Jimmy is still enthusiastic about working with horses.

"I'm very happy. If I had all the money in the world, I'd be doing exactly what I'm doing, and I'd work just as hard at it."

Jimmy's reputation is as a trainer, but buying and selling horses is still the main part of his business. Many trainers, he feels, just don't have enough knowledge about horses, and will unwittingly hurt good customers by selling them the wrong horse.

"You have to sell a horse to the person, no matter how much money he has to spend, according to the type of rider he is. If you oversell, the rider brings the horse's value right down to his level, and you've cheated him, but unintentionally."

Since he might have to buy at least five horses to come up with one good, saleable horse, Jimmy looks for horses "any place I can find them." He doesn't like to buy too many at the racetrack, however, and always looks into who did the training.

"If they've been shotgunned through the training to get them to the racetrack," he said, "they usually come out of it with a real bad attitude. And it's awfully hard to overcome that attitude because you can only train what a horse will give you mentally. They never forget their basic training. You're not looking for breeding because you don't care if they can run or not, and I'd rather have one that's not so pretty but has a calm, cool, and collected mind."

Currently about sixty students are in training at the Flintridge Riding Club. When talking about his philosophy of riding and training, Jimmy makes it simple: the way you can tell a good rider is if the horse likes him, or her. If the horse doesn't accept the rider—if he's sweaty and excited, fighting the bridle and switching his tail—then you know something is wrong. And ninety percent of it, Jimmy feels, is the rider's fault.

"People forget that horses aren't mechanical," he said. "They expect too much from the horse and from themselves. What you have to do is lower your IQ down to the horse's level and then bring the horse up gradually so the horse can understand. Most people will drive a horse crazy because they expect too much from him. Horses are big animals and they're slow thinking and frighten easily. If you surprise a horse or scare him, he will lose his mind."

Jimmy's students are trained the same way his horses are—slow and steady. A beginning rider is started out on a longe rein so that the instructor on the ground is always in control of the situation. The rider is taught how to sit in the saddle and is never frightened by the feeling of being out of control. In this way, the rider develops confidence in his or her ability to ride, and this confidence is transmitted to the horse.

It follows that a rider is never started over fences until he or she is perfectly secure on the flat: balanced and coherent with the motion of the horse. When a rider is preparing for competition, Jimmy expects to see him six days a week: "We take one day off to get our breath!"

Jimmy himself, however, has never had a formal lesson. He likes to call himself an experimentalist.

"I learned from everybody because I was eager to learn. I did a lot of things that were unorthodox, that my dad didn't approve of, but they worked."

But he doesn't claim that he figured everything out for himself. He has probably read every book that has been published on riding and training. And the bookcases in his living room crowded with horse books testify to that fact.

"I learned on my own because I studied. I really cared about what I did. And in those days," Jimmy remembered with a laugh, "anybody who read a book was considered stupid. Because in those days it was thought that 'those who could, did, and those who can't, read.' "

Jimmy does not limit himself to the books written by well-known riders and trainers, but will buy a book by a lesser-known writer as well, for the "opportunity to evaluate."

While Jimmy was called to the phone to discuss arrangements for giving a clinic, I talked with Susie Hutchinson, one of Jimmy's top assistants. Susie, now twenty-five, started riding with Jimmy when she was five and competed in her first show when she was six. She has been his teaching assistant now for the past six years. Susie rides her own horses (she currently has three). She takes care of office work in the mornings and teaches in the afternoons. She would like to be a trainer herself one day, and feels that her competing and instructing will be excellent background for it.

"I sometimes go to the clinics with Jimmy," Susie said, explaining her work, "and I ride or demonstrate or help instruct—whatever needs to be done. Here, Anne or Kappy {two other assistants} or I will sometimes get on a student's horse and school him.

"But as much as we can, we teach the kids to school their own horses. We try to stay off them. That's why it's important, as Jimmy said, to try to get horses to match the riders—or maybe get horses that are a little bit better than the riders, so they always have something to work for."

In addition to the horses owned by the students, Flintridge will take horses on consignment to sell. Once the students are riding their own mounts well, they are given the opportunity to ride these other horses. Part of the reason Jimmy's students are so accomplished is that they are able to ride several different horses.

Susie went on to explain that, unlike some trainers who demand rigid adherence to a particular riding style, Jimmy passes on his own individualistic approach to riding to his students.

"We let our kids develop their own styles, their own seats, to a certain extent," she said. "They're not stamped out with a certain way to do this or do that. We *do* want certain angles and so forth, but we just put the frosting on the cake."

Jimmy uses what he calls his "cowboy psychology" when he is teaching students. He gave as an example a student at one of his clinics who was trying to jump, but the horse kept knocking down the fence.

"You've told the student what to do," he said. "You go over it again and tell her again—everything you know is brought into it. But she still keeps knocking down the jump. The problem is that when she tries to do everything you've told her, she gets too rigid.

"So you say to the student, 'I'm upset with that horse you're on, embarrassing you like this. It's not your fault. Now I want you to ride him down to the fence so he'll really hurt himself. Don't do anything, ride him terrible, don't help him in any way.' And then the horse clears the fence! Because you've made the student relax.

"So cowboy psychology is doing the opposite. Have the

student tell you what the problem is, and what they've been doing about it, and then just tell them to do the opposite.

"I use this approach when I don't have any other input on the situation. In cases where you know the rider or the horse well, you have a better idea of what the problem is, and can come up with a solution."

Jimmy is not involved in eventing, but all of his horses, even the stock horses, learn dressage. Dressage, which comes from the French verb meaning "to train," is the art of training horses to perform all movements in a balanced, supple, obedient, and attentive manner. Jimmy believes it is the basic training of any horse. This also goes back to his philosophy that the sign of a good rider is a happy horse.

"The reason I like dressage," he said, "is that there are so many phases that keep the horse from being bored. If you can do the basic dressage movements, you can keep the horse happy.

"There are the lateral flexes, the shoulder-in, haunches-in, and two-track. And then you have the different rates of speed. For example, you've got the collected, working, medium, and extended trot.

"So it's like stretching a rubber band—the horse goes back and forth between your hands and legs. You move him up with your legs into the bridle and he accepts your hands.

"Your seat bone is the mediator. It's either complementary to your legs or to your hands. If your seat is complementary to your legs, you're accelerating. If your seat is complementary to your hands and the reins, you're retarding. So your seat and your weight influence are most important.

"Most people who read about dressage don't do the dressage, they do the *massage*. Their legs are too tight and they're pulling on the reins. They're clashing their aids and asking the horse to do something unnatural because they lack the balance and timing to coordinate with the horse."

Many horse people, Jimmy feels, knock dressage, but when you watch them schooling a horse you see that they are performing basic dressage movements. They do it from feel, because they are good riders. They might not know the names of the specific movements, but they are doing them just the same.

Jimmy studied dressage in Italy during World War II when he was with the 2610 Remount.

"The good Italians were supple," he said. "That's where I

Jimmy schooling a student

picked up a lot of my dressage and finesse. I had picked up a lot of the basic movements before I went into the army, because I was successful with horses, but I didn't know what to call it."

Jimmy oversees the daily activity of his club from a custom-made golf cart equipped with a stereo deck, siren, and loudspeaker. It can scoot down the aisles of the stables, and he can give instructions from it via the loudspeaker.

Jimmy has a reputation for adapting devices to use as teaching tools, or for inventing his own. The golf cart is one example; another is the elevator bit he developed, which lifts the horse's head and distributes the weight back onto the hindquarters.

"If you have a horse that's rank," he explained, "a child or a beginner can keep the horse's head up with the bit, which keeps the horse from ducking its head down and bucking them off."

Jimmy took me on a tour of the property from his golf cart. We passed several stables and open-air pens, and a number of riding and jumping rings. Riders of varying degrees of ability were schooling their horses or being given lessons. Everyone from the stablehands to the instructors to the students seemed relaxed and friendly and eager to share in Jimmy's sense of humor.

Grinning, he showed me his motto handed down to him from his father, which is written on the back of his truck: "It's what you learn after you know it all that counts."

"Once you think you know it all," he explained, "you're at a standstill."

Jimmy Williams, with his winning riders and horses, his curiosity, and his inventive mind, is definitely not at a standstill.

75

8
Show Rider

As a young girl growing up on a pony farm in Germantown, Tennessee, Melanie Smith always knew she wanted to work with horses. "But I certainly couldn't foresee," she said, "that I would be in the sort of position that I'm in now."

Her position is enviable: at twenty-nine she is one of the leading show jumping riders in the country, she rides for the U.S. Equestrian Team, and her show career is sponsored by Stillmeadow Farm in Connecticut, an operation she helped create.

Tired but cheerful after a demanding day of competition, Melanie was resting in the Stillmeadow exhibitor tent on the grounds of the AHRC (Association of Handicapped & Retarded Children) Horse Spectacular in Syosset, Long Island. Tanned, with sun-bleached hair and a smiling, friendly face, Melanie has the graciousness and easy manner one associates with the South. Making sympathetic grimaces each time the announcer's loudspeaker blasted through our conversation, she explained how her career as a show rider developed.

As she tells it, Melanie was raised on a farm that was

something of a miniature Noah's Ark. "We had geese and goats and sheep and chickens and all types of fowl and cows," she laughed. "It wasn't a large farm—we had just two or three of each animal."

The main activity of the farm revolved around the ponies. She rode her first pony when she was two, and has ridden almost every day of her life since.

"We had a riding school at our place and I would lead all the lessons," she said. "I would ride all the time. I rode in the Pony Club for about five or six years."

From the egg-and-spoon races, gymkhanas, and pole-bending contests of the Pony Club games, Melanie progressed to riding pony hunters and then to junior hunter and equitation classes in the South where she won the prestigious Mid-South Equitation Championship. It wasn't until she was nineteen and competing with her first jumper as an amateur owner that she began to show in the East.

It might be helpful here to clarify some horse show terminology. Competition is categorized by divisions. Each division is conducted according to the conditions and rules established by the American Horse Shows Association (AHSA).

A jumper may be any breed or height. The horse is judged solely on his ability to jump. Style and manner are not counted. The winner of a jumper division is the horse with the lowest number of faults or penalties. Time is sometimes a factor in deciding the winner. There is a wide variety of types of competition within the jumper division. For example, in some classes touches are penalized and in others the horse is faulted only if he knocks down an obstacle.

The hunter represents the type of horse used in the sport of fox hunting. He must have jumping ability, manners, style, and soundness. The judges are looking for a horse that has the ability to give the rider a comfortable, safe ride, along with the stamina to endure a long day's hunting, and the manners to make it enjoyable.

Hunters are divided into two main categories—working hunters and conformation hunters. The working hunter is judged solely on his performance and fitness. Conformation hunters must have looks as well as ability. They are usually judged sixty percent on their jumping performance and forty percent on their conformation. A green hunter is one in the first or second year of his show career. After two years he will move up to the regular hunter divisions where the fences are higher and more demanding.

In the equitation division it is the rider not the horse who is being judged. The rider is judged on hands, seat, and management and control of the horse. Junior divisions are restricted to riders who have not reached their eighteenth birthday. And pony classes are for animals measuring 14.2 hands (58 inches) or less.

When Melanie started showing on the eastern circuit, she came under the instruction of George Morris and received the first formal training of her show career. Her mother, whose background was in Western riding, taught her "how to stay on" and the basic equitation position.

"But as far as jumping and all that, I learned by the seat of my pants," she said. "I learned the natural way. I never really had any technical learning, except for reading books and a few lessons here and there, but no steady training until I rode with George."

Melanie has been training with George Morris since 1970, and she gives him credit for all of her open jumper training and knowledge. George's name is well known in show circles as one of the foremost instructor/riders on the circuit today. A former member of the U.S. Equestrian Team, he operates a show stable in Pittstown, New Jersey, and is busy throughout the year giving riding and teaching clinics across the country.

"He still helps me with the big Grand Prix classes and that sort of thing," Melanie explained. "I don't take lessons from him on a regular basis. I know I could get by without him if I had to, if I concentrate, but he gives me an extra edge."

She added with her easy laugh, "On the day that you think there's nothing left to learn you start to go down!"

Melanie, like many show riders, is still technically an amateur. She is careful to maintain and guard her amateur status so she will be able to qualify for Olympic competition.

"I can't accept money. I get my expenses paid and I have a place to live and wonderful horses to ride," she said, gesturing to the horses being bedded down in nearby stalls.

Melanie's relationship with Stillmeadow Farm developed when the owners, Mr. and Mrs. Neil B. Eustace, bought a hunter from Melanie for their daughter. They then became interested in jumpers and in sponsoring Melanie's career. They bought horses—including the two excellent performers Radnor II and Val de Loire—for Melanie to show. The Eustaces are mainly interested in supporting a sport that they enjoy, and the farm, according to Melanie, is not really a money-making enterprise.

"It's been a pretty good year this year," she said, "with the horses winning the Grand Prixes, but it's hard when you're carrying a lot of young horses—as we are—to win back your entry monies."

A good part of Melanie's time is spent training younger

Melanie Smith schooling a student before class

riders. When George is out of town she coaches his junior jumper riders. She also schools about eight horses on a steady basis for Stillmeadow and trains the Eustaces' daughter, who exhibits in the amateur hunter division. (And who, Melanie informed me with delight, had just won the last class of the day.)

Eventually, Melanie plans to turn professional.

"There is money to be made in the horse business, giving lessons and buying and selling horses," she explained. "Also, I think Grand Prix jumping is going to get larger and larger. They're trying to get it on television. I think that eventually we'll be able to see sponsorships and purses just like in tennis or golf. There are several people who have already signed contracts endorsing different products."

Melanie is right. Grand Prix jumping, the equivalent to Olympic class competitions sometimes referred to as the "big boy's" division, is one of the most difficult jumping events, as well as the most thrilling to watch. It may soon be on the air. International Management Group (IMG) was awarded exclusive TV rights for American Grand Prix jumping events and it is anxious to have them broadcast. Dave DeBusschere, former New York Knicks basketball star and IMG's senior vice-president, said recently: "We look forward to bringing the sport of show jumping to America's television public. We feel that the exposure will propel the sport as a major spectator event."

Melanie envisions her future career as a trainer, teaching young riders and schooling green horses.

"I like to teach, but only to a certain extent," she said. "Being on young horses—watching them progress, then selling them when they get to a certain level—that's what I really enjoy.

"It all goes along together—you build up the students and then they want to buy horses, so you have to have young horses coming along. I think it's important to do both: to be in the buying and selling, and also to be teaching. I'm sure that I will always be in the business in some way. I'd like to continue to show, and bring along young horses, and teach other kids as well. I think that people like myself, who've had good instruction and who've been successful, owe it to the business to help the young ones coming along by teaching and coaching them."

Much of what Melanie plans for her future she is doing now, but on an amateur basis—showing, coaching George Morris's students, training horses for Stillmeadow.

Her schedule is strenuous. The show season starts in Florida in February and continues through the six-day show at Madison Square Garden in November.

"We're on the road quite a bit," she said. "I try to rest the horses as much as I can. We'll show a couple of weeks and then we'll be home a couple of weeks. December and January are rest months. The show horses are completely let down. But I ride all the time."

A typical day at the farm in Stonington, Connecticut, starts with Melanie on her first horse by seven-thirty or eight in the morning. She rides, schooling horses, until four or five in the afternoon. Her show schedule, which often requires fourteen-hour days, is even more demanding. She begins coaching riders or schooling one of her horses at six in the morning. She schools, coaches, and shows all day, and often doesn't leave the grounds until eight o'clock at night. Traveling from show to show—packing, unpacking, feeding, training, trucking—is anything but glamorous.

"You have to love it!" she warned, laughing.

I asked what advice she would give to someone who wants a career as a show rider.

"Find a good place to take lessons. If you want to become a professional, you should get as much experience as possible and try to be as successful as you can in the junior hunter division. Get your name known competing as a junior. That's where you can find out if it's what you want—if you can handle the competition and pressure, and if you really enjoy it. The junior division is *very* competitive. So to me that's the best way to do it. Start as early as you can and get a good instructor."

Melanie stressed that you must compete at the big shows, and ride against the top people successfully, if you want a career as a professional rider. If you do and you do it well, it isn't difficult to find sponsors.

"But there are so many different facets," she added. "Not everyone has to be a good rider to be a good teacher, manager, or groom. Managing a show stable—making sure that the day-to-day requirements of the horses and personnel are met, scheduling the shipping of the horses, and making arrangements with the shows—is a full-time job. And good grooms are always in demand."

Other career possibilities in the show world are horse show judge, course designer, and show manager. In most cases, the people who hold these positions have distinguished themselves as competitive riders before moving to the other side of the fence.

Course designer Pamela Carruthers

The following morning, the day of the $10,000 Grand Prix class, Melanie was out early to coach the junior riders. Casually dressed in jeans and T-shirt and holding a can of soda, she stood by a schooling fence and called out instructions and criticisms to the riders. Finally, when the last one had been primed, she took one of her horses to a far corner of the field for some last-minute schooling of her own on the flat and over fences.

I found her later in the Stillmeadow tent polishing her boots and making a casual reference to a friend about a sash that she wasn't going to wear if she could help it.

"I don't really get nervous," she said in answer to a question. "I get excited. I get *up* for the class, but not nervous."

She was hard pressed to single out a highlight of her career, a particular show or event that meant more to her than the others. But the American Gold Cup in Philadelphia that she won with Radnor II in 1976 she remembers as "thrilling."

"That was the first really big class, the biggest money class, that I won. Anytime I win a Grand Prix or a really big class it's always equally as exciting as the time before. It never gets old—winning never gets old."

Later, at ringside, I understood her oblique reference to a sash as the show announcer informed the crowd of 10,000 spectators that Melanie Smith was wearing the white-and-blue leading rider sash, for accumulating more points than any other rider on the Grand Prix circuit.

Riding two horses, it looked as if she had a pretty good shot at this one, although several riders were on more than one horse. This particular class was an Olympic-qualifying

Melanie and Val de Loire clearing the last fence in the Grand Prix

event and had drawn international riders from Puerto Rico, Mexico, Canada, and Ecuador.

After the first round, both of her horses, Radnor II and Val de Loire, were still in the competition, but in the second round over a shortened and raised course, Radnor knocked down a rail and was eliminated. For the third and final jump-off against the clock, the course was shortened and raised again. There was only a handful of riders with perfect scores remaining from the original forty-odd. Racing against the clock, making impossible-looking turns down to truly enormous fences, rider after rider put in breathtaking rounds. A few, in their efforts to get the top speed, brought down rails to the groans of a sympathetic crowd. Melanie entered the ring and turned in a flawless round, knocking seconds off the best time. The ringmaster announced that she was now, with the fastest round, the rider to catch. No one did.

After the awards ceremony, she led the field of runners-up in a victory gallop around the ring. Several weeks later I watched her take another victory gallop. This time it was Madison Square Garden and Melanie had just been named Woman Rider of the Year. She was also awarded the prestigious title of Grand Prix Rider-of-the-Year for winning an unprecedented number of five Grand Prixes. Val de Loire was named Grand Prix Horse-of-the-Year. It marked the first time one horse-and-rider team had won all three titles. As the audience rose to its feet, applauding, Melanie's words came back to me: ". . . winning never gets old."

9
Groom

The duties of grooms, whether they are working with racehorses at the track, pleasure horses at a riding academy, or highly trained show horses, are pretty much the same. The basic care—feeding, rubbing, bandaging, and mucking out stalls—is universal.

The people filling the job, however, cover a wide range, all the way from young kids on summer jobs at a hack stable to old-time "lifers" at the track. Some enter the job as a life's work; others see it as merely a rung on a ladder. For most young people, the opportunities for experience and a chance to learn are the motives for keeping the job, rather than the salary, which usually ranges from $125 to $180 a week.

One of the least glamorous of the jobs working with horses, grooming does offer the most physical contact with the animal. Grooms, probably as no one else, are able to tell how their horses feel, emotionally and physically. From long hours of association with his or her horses, a groom is quick to spot potential trouble spots such as swelling or heat, and also knows when the horse is sulking because something is bothering him.

"The groom really knows the horse best," one exercise

rider at Belmont told me. "I'll always try to find out from the groom what kind of mood the horse is in before I take him to the track."

Jesse Michaels, a fifty-three-year-old veteran from Lexington, Kentucky, grew up in the business. His father had also been a groom. Jesse started working with horses as an exercise rider when he was thirteen. He moved around quite a bit, galloping horses at tracks in Kentucky, Ohio, and Florida before coming to New York. When he grew too large to continue riding ("Put on a few pounds," he admitted, patting his substantial girth), he started rubbing horses.

Jesse is the type of groom most trainers are looking for—conscientious and knowledgeable. For example, he knows just how much pressure is needed in a racing bandage, and will listen to the trainer's instructions and not improvise on his own.

"Your horses get to know you," Jesse told me. "They look for you and depend on you."

When asked what his job consisted of, he looked at me as if I were simpleminded and said, "I take care of my horses."

He has two horses in his charge, and taking care of them means just about everything: rubbing, washing, feeding, watering, bandaging—and soothing.

Jesse Michaels, with a rub rag dangling from his hip pocket and a hoof pick clipped to his belt loop, is the traditional old-time groom. He would never be happy in the quiet atmosphere of a breeding or training farm; he thrives on the excitement and goings-on at the track.

I also saw scores of young people working as grooms at the track, and many came from middle-class backgrounds

Groom giving a bath

and held college degrees. The days when many of the people who would take a grooming job were drunks and outcasts who couldn't find anything better to do are definitely a thing of the past.

Another groom I talked to, Jim Gordon, in his mid-twenties, has a degree in animal husbandry. He is working at the track to learn as much as he can about how thoroughbreds behave under the stress of racing before he takes a supervisory job at a breeding farm.

"You have to be conscientious," he said, explaining the requirements of the job. "If you agree to be at the barn at five-thirty, you have to be there—the trainer is depending on you, and so are your horses.

"You also have to be willing to learn and to take instruction. When I first took this job, I knew how to ride a horse but I didn't know anything more about taking care of them than knocking the dust off with a brush and cleaning out the feet with a hoof-pick.

"As for the job itself, I arrive at five-thirty every morning. I make a quick check of the horses, to make sure they've gotten through the night without trouble, then I start mucking out the stalls.

"The trainer arrives soon after I do and gives me the day's schedule. Then I get the horses ready to be walked around the shedrow, or galloped at the track, depending on what the agenda is for them for the day.

"I also take the horses' temperatures every morning. A lot of trainers do that just to be on the safe side, although I can usually tell from the feed tub and water bucket how the horses are doing. And once you know your horses, you can tell if they're sulking about something or not feeling well. Sometimes it might be a touch of colic. But other times you can't find anything wrong with them—I guess horses have their off days, just as we do.

"Most days I get off around noon. But if one of my horses is running, I'll stay for the afternoon to get him ready for the race and escort him over to the paddock. Then if we're lucky, I'll meet him again in the winner's circle to take him back to the barn.

"On other days if the trainer has to take one of his horses to another track, I'll stay here to oversee the afternoon chores for him. On the average, I'm here three or four afternoons a week."

In contrast to Jim Gordon, eighteen-year-old Maria Hernandez plans to make a career for herself as a racetrack groom.

"I really enjoy the work, even though the hours are difficult, and it's seven days a week, and when the weather's bad it goes right through to your bones," she said.

"I like working with horses, and it seems that every day you learn something new. For example, there are so many ways of treating a sore leg. I'm learning which treatment should be used, when, and why."

For most people, the early hours—from five to eleven in the morning, seven days a week, and afternoons when a horse is running—curtail any hopes for a "normal" social life since the day usually ends with bed at nine. But this is not a problem for Maria, who will soon marry an exercise rider who works for another stable.

"I suppose the only person I *could* marry would have to be involved with racehorses. Otherwise we'd never see each other."

Grooming is one of the best beginning jobs at the

racetrack. Because of the large turnover of help in a racing stable, good grooms are always in demand, but the long hours, hard work, and low pay are considerations that a prospective stablehand should weigh carefully before taking on the job.

Even so, you might decide, as Maria has, that it's one of the best places to be. "It's a good life. I like the people, I like the horses, and when one of my horses wins, it makes *everything* worthwhile."

Moving into the world of the show horse, you find much of the same excitement and pressures as at the racetrack.

Sharon McCormick, a nineteen-year-old originally from Ohio and now working on the East Coast, drifted into the horse show world last year when she took a summer job as a groom for a small show stable. The temporary job expanded, she became a full-time groom, and she now has no immediate plans for leaving.

"As with most of the people here," Sharon said, gesturing at the brightly colored tents of the Connecticut show grounds, "there were always horses around when I was growing up. My father claims that I knew how to ride before I could walk, and I played with toy horse statues instead of dolls.

"When I got out of school I was trying to decide what to do with my life, and I took a job grooming. I suppose I could have gotten a job somewhere as a riding instructor, but I would rather work with horses than with people. I still don't know what I'm going to do eventually, but right now I enjoy this."

Sharon paused to take out one of her horses that would be competing later. She put the gelding on cross-ties—chains with hooks on either end that attach to the opposite walls of the aisle between the stalls and hook onto the horse's halter, holding him straight in the center of the aisle.

"It's really not a bad life," she said, brushing the horse. "We're on the road a lot, which I enjoy. And there's a great feeling of camaraderie here. All the grooms are friends with the riders—and everyone else.

"When we're at a show I feed the horses at five so there will be plenty of time to get them ready for the first class of the day, which means grooming, braiding, and longeing. Usually they're given a good bath at home before we leave for the show, so once we're here they just have to be hosed down after each class, or at the end of the day. Keeping them shining is an all-year effort, which is why they look so good. You can't just arrive at a show and suddenly start brushing

Young horse handler at show

like mad. Regular care, the feeding, and their overall condition all contribute to making them look beautifully turned out in the class."

Indeed, the chestnut she was now going over with a rub rag was soon shining like a new copper penny.

"There are a lot of little secrets you learn that make the job easier," she said. "Like putting enough vinegar in the rinse water when you're washing the tail, to help take out the tangles, but not so much that the horse will smell like a salad. And putting a little blueing in the final rinse when you're washing white socks or gray horses. But the most important thing I do is give myself plenty of time. Whenever I rush, I'm bound to forget something. This way I always feel organized."

Once the horse was tacked up, Sharon led him over to the schooling area carrying a rub rag and fly sheet over her other arm.

"I take a cooler or a sheet with me to the ring in case the horse has to wait around for the class to begin, or if, after the class, he stays because it looks like he's going to be called back," she said. "It protects him from the sun and keeps him from getting a chill."

The rider took the horse to the schooling area to warm up and then returned to wait at the in-gate. Joking with the rider and wishing him luck, Sharon double-checked the tack to make sure everything was in place and gave the horse (and the rider's boots) a final once-over with the rub rag before they entered the ring.

When Sharon joined a group of onlookers at the in-gate, it was hard to tell who were the grooms, the trainers, and the out-of-uniform riders. It was, as she had said earlier, a tightly knit, friendly group.

10
Farrier

The farrier, also known as a blacksmith or horseshoer, is responsible for the care and treatment of the feet and lower legs of the horse. As such, he has one of the most vital professions connected with horses.

Horses wear shoes to protect their hooves. In some cases "corrective" shoes are used to rectify a faulty way of moving or an anatomy problem, or to restore the feet and legs from damage due to an injury or disease. The shoes wear down and must be replaced on a regular basis. In addition, the hoof is growing constantly, and must be filed down and reshaped every six to eight weeks. So even an unshod horse needs to see a farrier on a regular basis. If a horse is left unattended, the hoof will grow too long. This could result in the horse's stumbling, or forging at the trot (striking the front feet with the back feet). Overgrown feet also put an undue strain on the tendons and ligaments of the legs and may cause lameness.

Joe Harris, an easygoing, articulate man who has been shoeing horses in Virginia for the past nine years, credits his sister for his decision to become a blacksmith.

"Caroline always had a pony or horse around the house,"

he said, "and she spent every summer going off to local horse shows to ride in gymkhanas and Western pleasure classes. She usually dragged me along to be the chief groom, horse-holder, and rag-carrier. I never cared for riding myself; even today I only go on an occasional trail ride with my son and daughter. But I liked the excitement and the festive atmosphere of the shows.

"I always found myself drawn to the blacksmith's truck. The first time I watched a smith shoe a horse, I thought to myself, 'I can do that.' I've always enjoyed building things and working with my hands, and blacksmithing just immediately appealed to me. After I got out of school I decided to try my luck as a blacksmith."

Joe worked for two years as an apprentice to an experienced farrier. He followed the smith on his rounds, observing, learning, and gradually working on the horses himself.

"The first couple of months after I started out on my own were slow," he said. "Sometimes I would have only two or three jobs a day. But once I built up a clientele, and people were satisfied that I wasn't going to lame their horses, business picked up. You get a lot of jobs through word-of-mouth. Someone likes you and your work and tells her friend and so on. Now I have so many people coming to me to shoe their horses that I'm going all the time."

Literally working from dawn to dusk, Joe admits that the job can be strenuous. "I'll shoe maybe eight to ten horses a day, sometimes more if there's not too much traveling time involved. That's the thing in this business," he said, pointing to his specially equipped truck. "You have to travel from horse to horse, which cuts down on your working time. The old idea of the village blacksmith's shop is pretty much a thing of the past. Now we travel to the horses instead of the horses coming to us."

Joe charges $25 for a normal, straightforward shoeing, more (sometimes up to $70) if it involves corrective work, special pads, or tailor-made shoes. When I asked him about the difficulties of the job, he answered, "An aching back and rank horses."

"You're on your feet all the time and most of that time is spent crouching over the horse's foot. When you get a spoiled, rank horse, everything is harder. I'm never afraid of the horses; I've yet to meet one I can't handle. But it takes me two or three times longer to shoe a horse that's acting up."

Joe has had his share of mashed fingers, burns, bruises, and kicks, but shrugs them off as occupational hazards. As he points out, farriers don't have the best working conditions. Often you are working out of doors or in barns where there is no temperature control, so you feel the elements. You're hot in the summer, cold in the winter, and damp in the rain. There are also the normal distractions around a barn to contend with—other people, horses, dogs, cats, whatever, swirling around you as you work.

Contrary to popular belief, it does not take enormous physical strength to become a farrier, and many women have successfully entered the field. But a farrier must be willing and able to work hard, under trying conditions, for long periods of time. You must have at least average physical strength, good eyesight and hand-eye coordination, and hand and finger dexterity. A basic "feel" for animals and a good deal of common sense are also essential.

Wearing his leather work apron and heavy, steel-toed shoes, Harris picked up the right front foot of the horse he was about to shoe. In one swift, sure motion he placed it between his legs and held it in position with his knees. He proceeded to remove the old shoe.

"For most jobs," he explained, "I use keg shoes. They are machine-made and come in a multitude of shapes, sizes, weights, and materials. I like to work with a hot shoe. I find the alterations are easier and I can get a good fit, but some smiths prefer to use a cold shoe. I don't get into a lot of corrective work, although I do make handmade shoes for a couple of gaited horses I work on. To encourage them to keep up their high, animated gait you need weighted shoes, and the weights and balances are different for each horse. I make the handmade shoes from a metal bar stock. I might also do some special work, though not necessarily with handmade shoes, when I'm working with a veterinarian who wants a certain shoe or pad for a horse. For example, a horse recovering from founder (a very painful disease caused by swelling in the hoof) will need special shoes."

Aside from acquiring the basic skills of using the forge and blacksmith tools, a farrier must also have a thorough knowledge of the anatomy of the horse, particularly the workings of the tendons, ligaments, and joints of the legs.

As Joe said, "You have to know what a normal horse looks like—the natural balance standing and moving, the proper angles of the hoof and pastern, the structure of the foot and so forth, before you can correct any abnormalities. You must also know how to read x-rays and be familiar with medical terminology so you can understand the vet and the treatment he's asking for."

With the current horse population estimated in excess of 9 million, a person can make a very good living today as a

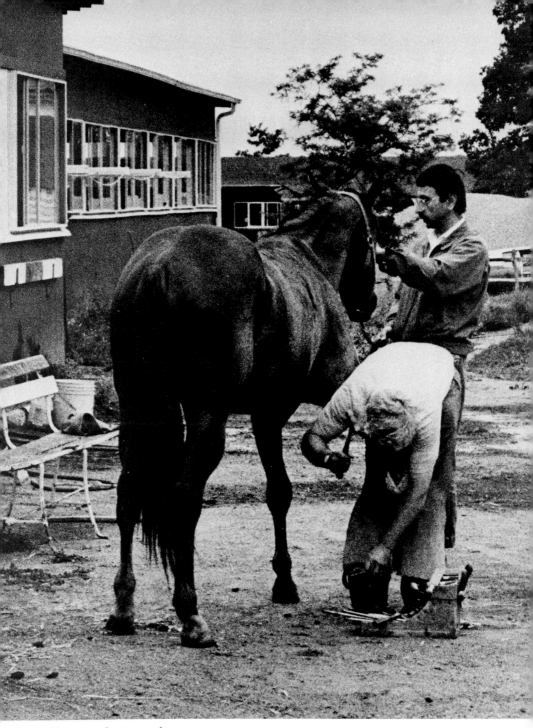

Farrier shoeing a horse

farrier. For those who want to be in business for themselves, it is a satisfying position. Incomes of $50,000 have been reported by farriers who are willing to put in eighty-hour weeks. The majority can work when they like, for as long as they like, on whatever days of the week they like. If you prefer, a limited number of salaried positions are available as resident farriers at some racing stables, and some breeding and show farms. Other farriers specialize in racetrack work and follow the circuit as race meets move from track to track.

The special knowledge and skills required to be a blacksmith may be learned by serving as an apprentice as Joe Harris did, or by attending one of the many horseshoeing schools across the country. The aim of the schools is to teach an overview of both the theory and practice of horseshoeing. During formal schooling, which consists of lectures, demonstrations, and actual hoof trimming and shoeing, you learn the basic skills of the trade, the proper use of the tools, and how to handle the horse and work with the horse owner. The better schools also offer instruction on animal psychology, public relations, professional image, business management, and the anatomy and physiology of the horse. However, completion of the course does not necessarily produce a completely skilled farrier ready to perform everything that is expected of a competent blacksmith. In fact, it is the opinion of many in the field, including Joe Harris, that the greatest value of the school is to shorten the time you will need to spend as an apprentice.

If you decide to go to a farrier school, write for brochures from as many farrier schools as possible. Carefully evaluate the schools to be sure that your time and money will be well spent. Unfortunately, many schools do not measure up to their claims, and produce ill-trained graduates. Some important criteria to take into consideration are the ratio of students to instructors, the number of horses actually shod during the course, the ratio of time spent in forge work to time spent trimming and shoeing, and the depth of theory taught in such important areas as horse anatomy, physiology, psychology, and disease. If possible, talk to graduates from the school, and check the backgrounds of the instructors. Are they people who have just taken a course, or are they experienced farriers? Above all, a correspondence course, a three-to-five-day "short course," or a clinic cannot be considered viable training.

"Shoeing a horse is really a fine art," says Joe Harris. "If you don't know what you're doing you could easily make a mistake that will lame the horse. You owe it to yourself and to your customers to get the best education possible."

As for precareer training, working with horses or other animals in any capacity provides a valuable background, as does working with hand tools such as files, hammers, and chisels. High school shop courses or vocational school courses in hot metal working or blacksmithing are particularly helpful. Other related courses you can take that will aid in giving you a good foundation for farrier work are physical science, anatomy, public relations, and basic business management.

11
Mounted Police

The sight of a cop on a horse patrolling city streets offers a refreshing contrast to the steel and concrete surrounding him. Mounted units, which were eliminated or drastically cut back with the advance of modern technology, are experiencing a revival in police departments across the country. Once assigned almost exclusively to city parks, the mounted police now work high crime areas, and their success in such cities as Philadelphia, New York, Chicago, St. Louis, and Boston has proved that the horse is a valuable member of the police team and an important asset to any modern city.

Many of the problems that confront today's police are effectively met by the return of the horse. For one thing, an officer on a horse is more accessible to the general public than an anonymous face in a squad car. In fact many passers-by find it almost impossible *not* to approach a mounted officer, if only to ask the horse's name, age, and breed. The resulting friendly conversation goes a long way toward improving the poor public image that has troubled police departments over the past years.

In addition to enhancing public relations, a mounted officer has greater visibility and capabilities than a footman.

He can see and be seen, which is in itself an important crime deterrent. But while there are obvious advantages in employing horses for patrol work, it is in crowd control situations that they are particularly useful. In a potentially dangerous crowd a horse and rider can do the work of ten footmen with minimum violence—it is far easier to move someone with half a ton of horse than with a night stick. Indeed, says police officer Dino Martini of the New York City Mounted Division, in some situations the people move before you get there.

"The sight of you coming at them will move them," he explains, "so you have minimal physical contact. You don't have the hand-to-hand situation that you have with foot patrolmen, and this eliminates a lot of injuries on both sides."

Dino joined the New York police in 1967 after putting in a four-year hitch with the navy. He spent his first year as a member of the Tactical Patrol Force (TPF). The primary focus of the TPF is on disorders that occur in congested inner-city areas. It is an active unit, with its members often working out of uniform and using their own cars as a base of action. Because of the high potential for danger and the involvement in "heavy" police work, the officers are generally given preference over other applicants when they are ready to switch to another unit. After a year Dino requested mounted.

"I can't say I always dreamed of being a mounted cop," he said, "but once I joined the police I liked what I saw of the mounted when they were on patrol or working at various demonstrations. I also liked the public relations aspect—the idea of breaking the communication barrier with the people. Radio cars tend to be objects that stand between the police officer and the public, whereas the horse contributes to a natural flow of conversation. And you have a mobility that a footman doesn't have.

"When you talk about crowd control or street crime prevention, the horse is invaluable. There is a lot of weight and power in a horse; with a man sitting on him, it's a large, awesome unit. Most city dwellers don't know horses, so the element of uncertainty is there. They don't know what the horse is going to do, but usually a horse won't step on a person. They want to step on something solid that will support their weight. However, someone could get clipped by a hoof if the horse steps over them."

Dino stated that the horses were important during the demonstrations of the Vietnam era in controlling unruly crowds and in lessening violent confrontations. In such situations, traditional formations which date back to European calvary schools such as the flying wedge and echelon are employed to clear the way for officers on foot. Well-trained horse-and-rider units are also effective in handling spontaneous outbreaks. He remembered one incident at a rock concert at Madison Square Garden in which a crowd suddenly got out of hand when it discovered there were no more seats. The guards were quickly overwhelmed by the angry protesters and they summoned the mounted patrolmen stationed outside the arena for help. The police officers rode into the rather large lobby with their horses and the people immediately dispersed.

In a similar situation, Dino came to the aid of two patrolmen trying to stop a fight in a hotel in the theater district.

"About thirty people were fighting in the lobby of a third-rate hotel," he said. "They were breaking up the place. Furniture was flying and the patrolmen were swamped. One of them opened the door for me and I rode the horse right up the steps and into the lobby. Everything immediately stopped as the people rushed to get out of the way of the horse."

He went on to explain that just as the unit of man and horse impresses the civilian, it also affects the mentality of the officer.

"The fact that you are on a horse makes you forget your vulnerability," says Dino. "For example, one time I chased an armed man who had just robbed a bank. I had no reservations about approaching him on the horse with my gun drawn and ordering him to drop his weapon. He did. Had I been a footman or in a patrol car, I know I would have been behind something. A car, a mailbox, anything. But on a horse you just don't think of that.

"I don't know," he said, laughing at himself, "maybe I've seen too many westerns. But it works both ways. A crazy-looking mounted cop cantering toward you and sliding to a stop on the sidewalk in front of you—you'd drop a rifle if you had it.

"It's that element of fear that makes a mounted cop a big deterrent to street crime. Because of our size we can be seen by the potential perpetrator of a crime. We can also look over the heads of the crowd to see what is going on."

When they are not being used for special events or demonstrations, the Mounted Division either walks to or is vanned to all areas of the city for patrol. They work the tough precincts of Harlem, midtown, and the garment district. They are also well suited for the narrow streets and heavy pedestrian traffic of Wall Street and Greenwich Village.

In order to get into mounted a police officer must have a good arrest and work record. Because it is a highly specialized and desirable unit, there is usually a waiting list for admission. You don't need a knowledge of horses; you'll get that at Remount. But if you're applying for the job and do have riding experience it will give you an edge. Currently the division is all male although until recently they had two women on the force.

The fiscal crisis in New York a few years back threatened to end the mounted unit. It was saved in part by making a nationwide appeal for the donation of horses. As a result, the eighty-four horses now on the force represent nearly every breed and type, from Thoroughbred to Quarter Horse to Appaloosa. A generous Texas oil magnate donated twenty Tennessee Walking Horses.

Police horses are at least 15.3 hands and geldings. Just like any other recruit, they must first pass a medical. Then they are sent to Remount where they are tested for suitability for the job. A successful street horse is obedient and unflappable. Training takes from one to three months depending on prior experience, intelligence, and temperament. In most cases the officers themselves school the horses.

Once a horse is accomplished at the gaits and responsive to the signals of his rider, the real test comes. He is subjected to simulated urban conditions—a circling patrol car with siren blasting and light flashing, the sound of pistol fire, and even a fake raucous crowd. A horse who passes reasonably unshaken is ready for patrol work.

Not all successful graduates are suitable for street work, however. Dino cited as an example his first mount, a big mixed-breed horse named Roland. As is custom, Dino would tie Roland in a garage when he went on a meal break.

Dino Martini on patrol

Inevitably he would come back to find the horse standing with the saddle twisted sideways or underneath him and the bridle lying on the floor.

"Roland was a good police horse," says Dino. "His only drawback was that he just didn't like the tack the way it was, and he was constantly rearranging his saddle and slipping out of his bridle."

Roland was eventually thrown off the force.

Police horses are assigned to the one officer who is their regular rider and who oversees their care. The horses are on a routine maintenance schedule and receive regular visits from a veterinarian and farrier. They are wormed three times a year and have their teeth floated (filed down) at least once a year. One of the biggest problems is foot strain. Rubber shoes were tried to ease concussion, but were discarded for all but a few horses. According to Dino, they are difficult to fit and tend to break apart easily. Many horses have corrective shoeing to offset navicular strain, and most of them have borium studs on their shoes to prevent slipping on the concrete streets. Because the horses receive such good care—clean and airy stabling, proper feed and moderate exercise—they average twelve years on the force. This is certainly longer than the life span of a patrol car. When they are ready for retirement, the horses are sent to an ASPCA-run farm where they are used as blood donors for producing serum.

Reflecting on his career, Dino said he always liked horses, but never had a chance to ride when he was growing up in New York. Once he joined mounted, he developed a deep interest in the art of riding.

"I feel that to be an efficient mounted cop one should develop a high degree of proficiency on a horse," he said, "more than your average rider. Dressage-type riding lends itself to police work because the difficult maneuvers like passing, two-tracking, turning on the fore, turning on the hind, and so forth, are necessary for mobility in crowd control. Dressage also promotes a good discipline between horse and rider and that is essential to our type of work. You get a basic dressage training at Remount, but to continue it you have to pursue it on your own. There really isn't time or manpower for refresher courses."

Dino enjoys his job and plans to stay in the Mounted Division until he retires from the force. He has helped train new officers and has taught riding on a limited basis off the job. He has even taught his two daughters to ride. Once he retires he would like to continue working with horses and he hopes to operate a small barn where he can raise and train horses. His plans are far from definite at this point, but he is thinking of concentrating on Morgans or Appaloosas, two breeds he particularly admires.

One of the highlights in mounted is the annual sixteen-man musical ride at the horse show in Madison Square Garden. I talked to Dino and others backstage at the Garden where they were rubbing horses that were already shining and flecking imagined specks of dust from their well-polished boots. Unlike the famous Canadian Mounties, which is strictly an exhibition unit riding specially bred horses, "New York's Finest" are working mounted patrolmen who train on their own time to perfect their ride at the Garden. They are one of the star attractions of the show. The event is a good morale builder for the entire department and a strong motivation for the men to keep up their riding edge. Looking dashing in their dress blues as they cantered and galloped through intricate formations, their spirit and enthusiasm soon infected the huge audience which was clapping and cheering in time to the music.

12
Rodeo Rider

Rodeo in the western states is a way of life. Over the past twenty years it has emerged into a major competitive event with the color, pageantry, and prize money that would make an old-time cowboy rub the trail dust from his eyes in disbelief.

The word "rodeo" comes from the Spanish word for roundup. No one knows where the first rodeo was held, but one legend puts it at Deer Trail, Colorado, in the late 1870s. The contestants were cowboys from the Hashknife, Campstool, and Mill Iron ranches. During a rest taken when their herds converged on a drive to the north, the toughest men and the toughest horses from each outfit matched for a test of skill and bravery. Competitions of this sort at the end of the long trail drives quickly caught on. In 1883 the town of Pecos, Texas, offered prize money for a steer-roping contest. Five years later a Denver, Colorado, rodeo charged admission for spectators, and rodeoing became a full-fledged business.

In the early rodeos, cowboys risked life and limb for little more than enough money to reach the next town, fairground, or stockyard. Today the Professional Rodeo Cowboys Association holds over 600 rodeos annually with more than seven million dollars offered in prize money. In addition, hundreds of smaller, unsanctioned rodeos are held each year across the country. Most rodeos have special events for cowgirls, such as barrel racing. There is also a Girls Rodeo Association (GRA) that holds all-girl rodeos. Members of the GRA risk their necks on broncs and bulls as bravely as the men. On a younger level, there are intercollegiate rodeos and interscholastic contests for high school students. Rodeo even has its own Little League, called Little Britches, for boys and girls from eight to eighteen.

Events in today's rodeo have evolved out of the way of life in the old West. In the days when cattle ranches spread from Texas to Montana, cowboys made their living herding cattle down from winter pastures each spring so that the calves could be roped, branded, and altered into steers. They then tended the enormous herds until the annual fall round-up when the cattle were driven north to railroad depots.

Ranch life was demanding and hard. Each cowboy needed a string of horses and no one had the time for the niceties of schooling a green horse. Untamed horses would be lassoed, thrown to the ground, and saddled. The cowboy would then climb aboard and attempt to hang on through the wild bucking until the horse—or the cowboy's back—was "broken."

Thus two of the standard rodeo events, calf roping and saddle bronc riding, have their origins in actual ranch work.

Calf roping, in which the contestant ropes and ties a calf as if preparing it for branding, requires precision skill with a rope and a well-trained horse. A calf is given several seconds' head start out of the chute before the cowboy gallops after it. The cowboy lassos the calf and quickly secures the other end of the rope around his saddle horn. As soon as the calf is lassoed, the horse slides to a stop and backs, keeping the line taut to restrain the calf. The cowboy then jumps from the saddle, races to the calf, and flips it on its side. He ties three legs together with a pigging string (a short length of rope) which he has been carrying in his teeth. The contestant with the fastest time wins, but if the calf breaks free from the pigging string before five seconds have elapsed, the round is automatically disqualified.

Saddle bronc riding is reminiscent of the methods used to break untamed horses. The saddle used in this event is a modified stock saddle, smaller and without a horn. A leather flank strap is also tightened around the horse's flank just before the chute is opened to encourage good bucking action. Before the ride begins the cowboy lowers himself onto the back of the horse in the starting chute. He holds on to a rope attached to the horse's halter. He must not touch the animal with his free hand during the ride or he will be disqualified. Once he is ready he signals for the gate to be opened and the horse explodes into the arena in a bucking frenzy. The ride must last ten seconds to qualify. If the rider is still on when the buzzer sounds, one of two "pick-up" men will gallop up to help him dismount. The other pick-up rider releases the flank strap, which stops the horse's bucking.

Two judges award points from zero to twenty-five on the cowboy's performance. A separate score from zero to twenty-five is awarded for the horse's performance. The rider with the highest total score wins. For this reason cowboys hope to draw difficult horses (the animals are selected by lottery), which they refer to as "money" horses.

The average four-day rodeo requires sixty-five to seventy bucking horses. These horses come from a number of sources. When a rancher finds he has a horse that is an "outlaw"—a horse that is unbreakable—he may sell him to the rodeo. Some bucking horses are just plain mean and ornery. They will look for every opportunity to kick or bite. Others will eat out of a child's hand while in the paddock but turn into a bucking tornado when a contestant mounts him in the rodeo arena. A problem rodeo stockmen have is finding a good horse that will buck with an experienced rider. They will throw an amateur quickly, but once an experienced rider shows he knows what he is doing they will stop bucking and start running around.

One thing bucking stock—horses and bulls—have in common is that they will do just about the same thing every time they come out of the chute. After a cowboy draws his rides, he will try to find others who have ridden the animals before so they can tell him what to expect.

The other three events that are rodeo classics are bareback bronc riding, bull riding, and steer wrestling, also known as bulldogging.

Bareback bronc riding requires strength, balance, and skill. The rider can only use one hand to hold the grip which is attached to a strap around the horse's girth. Eight seconds is the time limit. There is a good chance for injury riding these horses. The surging back and forward motion of the buck tends to tear up the rider's elbow as well as the hand itself. Spurring on the horse's shoulders, necessary to win points from the judges, is rough on the knees. Riding rodeo stock is an injurious profession. You get hurt a little bit every time you come out of the chute even if you don't get in a "wreck."

Bull riding is the ultimate danger. Bulls will turn and try to gore a thrown rider, and they are so big and strong that they can send a rider flying if they just brush up against him. The horns of rodeo bulls are blunt, but if they get a solid shot at your chest they're going to break ribs.

A bull is ridden with what is called a bull rope that goes around his middle with a weighted bell on the bottom. The rider tightens the bull rope around the bull's chest, depending on how strong he thinks the bull is. A bull's muscles swell tremendously when he explodes out of the chute. If the rider has taken too tight a hold, the bull will snap the rope right out of his hand. The time limit is eight seconds.

In steer wrestling, the steer is released from the pen with the cowboy and another rider, called a hazer, in hot pursuit. The hazer rides along the other side to keep the steer straight. When the cowboy is level with the steer's head he flings himself from the saddle, grabs the animal's horns, and digs his feet into the ground. With his arms wrapped in a deadlock on the steer, he then wrestles it onto its side. All this must be accomplished in less than five seconds if the cowboy expects to get a share of the prize money.

Some of the larger rodeos feature other events. In a popular competition, a horse-and-rider team separate a calf from a herd, then the horse works to keep it from returning to the group. The horse, called a cutting horse, must perform with no visible assistance from his rider. A good cutting horse will have complete control of the cow, taking it a distance from the others so as not to disturb the herd. The horse should anticipate and react swiftly to the cow's every move, working her tightly; that is, not running the cow from wall to wall. Each horse is given two and a half minutes to perform. Time starts when the horse's name is

114

announced, and the rider works as many cattle during that period as he sees fit.

Another exciting event is team roping. One rider, the "header," lassos the steer around the head or horns, secures the rope to the saddle horn, and pulls the steer aside so the "heeler" can lasso the heels. Once the heeler has secured his rope to the saddle, both riders turn their horses toward each other, with the steer in the middle, and signal that they are finished. Again, the fastest time wins.

Some rodeos feature wild and colorful chuck wagon races. Teams of four or six horses pull wagons around a track in a madcap race. There might also be exhibitions of trick riding, fancy roping, or musical rides. There is usually a parade with a rodeo queen and her court.

Professional rodeo cowboys, and cowgirls, are a tough and hardy lot. It is a bruising and exhausting way of life. Modern rodeo, sometimes called the suicide circuit, subjects a performer to pressures the old working cowboys never knew. His body is subjected to almost constant abuse since he must compete in as many rodeos as possible in pursuit of purses. This involves traveling hundreds, sometimes thousands, of miles to get from arena to arena. He stays on the road for months at a time. Most cowboys enter at least a hundred rodeos a year if they want to make real money. Tom Ferguson, the first rodeo performer to top $100,000 in a year ($30,000 is impressive), tries to hit 120 rodeos. To do this he may enter two, sometimes three, rodeos at once, geography and time permitting.

Tom is something of an idol to aspiring young rodeo riders. He has taken the World All-Around Championship, for which a cowboy must earn money in at least two events, five straight times. A handsome young man in his twenties,

Tom is a gifted athlete with split-second reflexes. He competes in calf roping and steer wrestling. At 5′ 11″ and 180 pounds, he is smaller than most steer wrestlers. But countless hours of practice and conditioning make him a marksman with his rope and enable him to upend a steer with ease. Another ingredient of his success is that he is a positive thinker who sees no sensible reason for failure.

When he is not on the road, he and his wife live in a modest bungalow in Miami, Oklahoma. But when he is on tour they travel in a custom-built trailer complete with its own water supply and generator to supply electricity. It features a bathroom with a shower, a kitchen, comfortable beds, and air conditioning. There is storage space for saddles, bridles, and ropes plus a rear stable for three horses and their feed.

Tom, like many of the new breed of cowboy, has a college education. While in high school he practiced every night in his father's back lot catching calves and jumping steers. He was the amateur calf roping champion in his senior year in high school, and he won a scholarship to the California Polytechnic Institute at San Luis Obispo. When he went to college he took six steers, ten calves, and a roping horse with him to enable him to keep practicing and competing in amateur rodeos.

Calm and easygoing, Tom tries not to let the pressures and setbacks of rodeo life affect him. After narrowly missing a $15,000 first place in a calf roping contest when his rope broke, he took the loss in stride. "The best thing about rodeo," he said, "—or maybe it's the worst—is that there's always another one."

Young hopefuls who want to attain Tom's status may attend clinics given by former rodeo champions to improve

Rodeo rider roping a calf

their skills. One ex-champion, Larry Mahan, puts his students on real broncs, explaining that the animals don't know or care that they are being ridden by beginners. It is a system that does encourage one to learn quickly.

However, most clinics and clubs use sophisticated training aids such as the "El Toro"—an electronic bucking machine used by hundreds of colleges, schools, and rodeo clubs across the country. Another popular machine, the Gold Nugget Rider Trainer, is a fiberglass beast designed to duplicate the action of a bucking horse or rodeo bull.

Before technology made the development of these sorts of machines possible, early bronc riders practiced on homemade "bucking barrels," which were kegs hung from barn ceilings or tree limbs by ropes or springs. They were yanked about in all directions by enthusiastic helpers in an effort to simulate bucking horses and bulls.

More and more women are performing in the Girls Rodeo Association which was organized in Pecos, Texas, in 1947. In the men's rodeo, cowgirls are limited to performing in the barrel racing event. Three fifty-gallon oil drums are positioned to form a triangular course. In a race for the best time, horse and rider gallop a cloverleaf pattern around the barrels (without turning them over). More than eighteen seconds is a slow score.

In the girls' rodeo, contestants may enter the bareback bronc riding, bull riding, barrel racing, calf roping, goat tying, steer undecorating, and team roping events.

The bucking stock that the women ride is not as tough as the men's, and the time limit is reduced to six seconds. But it is a dangerous profession nevertheless and more than one cowgirl has been stomped on by a frenzied horse or narrowly escaped the horns of an angry bull. On both the bulls and the broncs the women have the option of riding with one or two hands.

The goat tying contest is similar to the men's steer wrestling. The goat is tied to a stake with a ten-foot rope in the middle of the arena. The cowgirl gallops up to the goat, throws it to the ground, and ties three legs together with the pigging string. Fastest time wins.

In steer undecorating a cowgirl and her hazer gallop out in pursuit of a steer, and the cowgirl leans over and snatches a ribbon off the steer's shoulder. If she wants part of the prize money she must be able to grab the ribbon within two to three seconds.

Team roping is the same as the men's event. In fact, a cowgirl can compete in the men's rodeo in team roping—if she has a male partner.

The cowgirls who follow the rodeo circuit do so for many of the same reasons as the men: the hope of striking it rich (though only a small percentage of the performers make real money and the purses in the girls' rodeo are much smaller than the men's), the pursuit of the coveted "Champion" title, the thrill of competing in dangerous and exciting events, and a desire to be on the road.

The cowboys and cowgirls who perform in the rodeo are carrying on a unique and distinctly American tradition. The essence of the rodeo—the spirit of competition and the footloose hardihood of the riders—has remained unchanged since it first began in dusty little towns over one hundred years ago.

13
Breeding Farm

Horse-related activities—racing, showing, rodeo, pleasure riding—are enjoying an upsurge, with the result that there is an ever-increasing demand for more horses. And the demand is not just for more horses, but for carefully bred horses. Popular breeds such as the Thoroughbred, Arabian, and Quarter Horse are more in demand than ever before. To use the Quarter Horse as an example, in one year there were 500,000 *new* Quarter Horse owners. And that's just one breed. Other breeds that were once rare in this country, such as Andalusians and Trakehners are now found in larger and larger numbers. It is the job of the breeding farms to meet this growing demand for horses and to preserve what is special about the breeds.

The jobs available on a breeding farm are much the same as at any large stable: grooms, trainers, stable managers, foremen, and exercise people. The big difference is that breeding farms, unlike other stables, are almost totally dependent on foal production and stud fees for income. Success in managing the stallions, mares, and foals determines the life or death of the farm. On the smaller farms the line between profit and loss is perilously thin. At the bigger operations there is more of a margin for error.

For obvious reasons, farm workers who develop a knowledge and skill in breeding procedures are very valuable. This expertise may be the ticket to a specialized job such as stud manager.

A stud manager is a specialist in breeding procedures. He or she must have a sound knowledge of genetic prepotency, which is the ability of a horse to pass on to his offspring the particular characteristics that make him special, such as beauty, speed, and temperament. A stud manager must also be familiar with estrous cycles and know when a mare is physically capable and ready to breed. An awareness of the fertility problems that may arise is also part of the job.

However, the primary concern of a stud manager is the handling of the stallions with an eye toward getting the highest possible stud fees. Two important factors affect the value of a stallion: his reputation and performance, and the reputation and performance of his get, which is what his offspring are called.

Managing a successful stallion can be highly profitable. One Standardbred stakes winner was retired to stud in 1970 with a $2,000 standing fee. His popularity soon upped the figure to $4,000, then to $5,000. Now, as a "proven" stud, he commands a $10,000 stud fee. With a schedule of covering 200 mares, he earns $200,000 a year.

The selection of the right mare plays an important role in the breeding game. Breeding experts carefully pore over the genetic and performance history of both the stallions and the mares in hopes of coming up with the perfect "nick"— the chromosome chemistry between a mare and a stallion that produces a winning foal.

But there are no sure things in this business. Mating the

fastest stallion to the speediest mare does not guarantee a stakes-winning colt, though your odds are good. There is always the inexplicable Cinderella horse with no background to speak of, no champions on either side, who outshines his better bred peers.

One of the unforeseen hazards is the shy breeder. This is often the case when a young, inexperienced stallion has been intimidated by a stressful racing career or show schedule or by the use of drugs. Some breeders successfully overcome this problem by putting the stallion in the constant presence of an experienced, inexpensive crossbred mare. Provided with easy access to the mare, sharing a paddock or an extra large stall, he usually overcomes his shyness.

In a normal breeding process, a mare in estrus is brought into the breeding barn to be "teased" by the stallion which usually means some snorting and neck biting. For this stage they are physically separated by a stall wall or door. Once the mare signals her readiness to accept the stallion's advances, she is washed and her tail is wrapped. She is then taken to the breeding area where she is presented to the stallion. Since the washing has taken a few moments, she may have cooled down and needs to be teased again. The mare is then bred to the stallion under the careful observation and handling of the breeding crew. After the mating, the mare is returned to her stall, or to a waiting van if she has come in from another farm. The whole procedure takes about fifteen minutes.

The stallions being bred do not always tease their own mares. Some stud managers prefer to use a surrogate stallion for teasing in order to save time and conserve the stallion's energy. They might only have the stallion tease his mares once or twice a week during the busy breeding months.

Other managers prefer to use the stallion through the whole process for libido and disciplinary reasons.

For a close-up look at a breeding operation, I traveled to Ocala, Florida. Everywhere bumper stickers can be seen proudly announcing that "Ocala is Affirmed Country." The popular Triple Crown winner, Affirmed, was bred and raised on one of Ocala's 185 Thoroughbred breeding farms. But Thoroughbred breeders aren't the only ones to take advantage of the climate and grazing conditions that make the area excellent horse country. Numerous Tennessee Walker, Morgan, Arabian, Quarter Horse, and Appaloosa breeding farms can be found throughout the region.

My destination was Nodoroma Farms, an Arabian horse operation. My choice of Arabians as an example of a breeding farm seemed particularly apt to me since the Arabian is the oldest breed of horse. The characteristics of the breed—its stamina, courage, easy adaptability, speed, gentleness, and great beauty—have been preserved in a selective breeding heritage that dates back over thousands of years. The slogan of Nodoroma Farms, "Quality for the Future," promises to uphold that tradition.

Spread over 285 acres of what was once a Thoroughbred farm, Nodoroma is a picture of tranquility. On every side of the long road winding down and around to the main stable are pastures of horses apparently separated according to their breeding status. The stallions, because of their highly competitive and bellicose nature when surrounded by mares, are put in their own paddocks. Mares in foal are separated from the mares with young colts and fillies at their sides. Likewise, groups of yearling colts and fillies are each in their own pastures.

In the main stable I watched a young man training a yearling to stand in the position required in halter classes—all four feet square with the head and tail held high. It seemed a tedious process. Each time the man put tension on the lead shank, asking the filly to extend her head and neck, she took a step forward. Finally, he snapped the longe whip on the ground with a loud crack that sent her rearing backward.

"It sounds a lot worse than it is," said Mrs. Murch. Wife of Halsey Murch, manager and trainer, Mrs. Murch had offered to take me on a tour of the farm. "He's just trying to get her attention."

I mentioned that it seemed to take a lot of patience to train a young horse. She heartily agreed. Since success in the show ring greatly enhances the reputation of a farm and leads to high stud fees for the stallions and saleable foals, training is an ongoing process.

There are approximately one hundred horses at Nodoroma and the farm averages a sale of fifteen horses a year. The prices of show caliber and fine breeding horses range between $20,000 and $30,000, but those looking for reasonably priced well-trained show and pleasure horses can also be accommodated. On the current sales list of forty-three horses you find a complete range, from a $1,500 yearling colt to a $50,000 pure Polish mare. The owners, Mr. and Mrs. Norman Sauey, started the farm with a foundation stock of domestic bred Arabians which included several of the old Egyptian lines. Always searching for horses to improve and preserve the quality of the herd, Mr. Sauey traveled to the Polish Arabian auctions held in Poland and Sweden in 1977. He brought back six horses, including two stallions.

Nodoroma mare and foal

Mrs. Murch took me to visit the current foal crop, several of which had been sired by the new stallions. I couldn't tell the difference between a domestic, an Egyptian, or a Polish line Arabian (there are evidently ardent supporters of each type), but the foals were magnificent. I was impressed by their beauty and how well they represented their breed. They all looked like they were supposed to—fine-chiseled heads, large expressive eyes, and arched tails. I was also struck by the gentleness of the mares, who allowed us into the stalls with their foals without protest. Mrs. Murch pointed out one of the mares and her foal who had just been sold as a package deal. Twenty-five years old, the mare had been one of the foundation stock.

Deryl Duncan, the stud manager, arrived with the vet, who administered a worming solution to the foals. A big, strong-looking, dark-haired young man, Deryl is a Nodoroma success story. He started out on the farm as a groom and worked in every capacity. Now thoroughly versed in the operation of the farm, he takes over management of the daily operation when necessary. It is also his responsibility to make sure all goes smoothly when the horses are at a show. He supervises setting up the stalls and the elaborate show decorations and is constantly on hand to prevent potential problems from developing. The job is rigorous since classes might go on until eleven o'clock at night and he is up at dawn to oversee the feeding and grooming.

Quiet and serious, he wasted no motion as he escorted the vet on his rounds of the farm. But they met a stumbling block when they tried to bring one of the pregnant mares in from the field for a shot. Acting as if it were all an elaborate game, the mare allowed the men to come within inches of

126

her head before turning tail and slipping tantalizingly out of reach. She then pretended to fall for the grain-in-the-bucket routine before taking off in a gallop. The rest of the mares followed and they raced at breakneck speed up the hill, through the trees, and back.

I was concerned that pregnant mares should behave in a more docile manner. But they kicked up their heels and nipped at each other like yearlings. One of the galloping mares had recently been sold to a breeder in Australia. The shipping alone, by air via England and a long quarantine, would cost $10,000. She was in foal and the new owner hadn't yet decided whether to ship her or wait until the foal was born.

Deryl Duncan with pregnant mare and her foal

Deryl and the vet decided to forget the mare for the time being and they strode off for the breeding barn where another mare was being prepared to be bred.

When contemplating what careers were available in the breeding field, Mrs. Murch offered Deryl as an example. Deryl at one time had expressed an interest in becoming a trainer, but he discovered his talent lay in the breeding end of the business. He is now in charge of the Nodoroma breeding program and the farm recently sent him to Colorado University for their course in artificial insemination. Artificial insemination, not permitted in some breeds, is accepted by the Arabian Horse registry.

According to Mrs. Murch, a breeding farm offers good long-term opportunities for someone interested in a career as a farm manager or stud manager. On a small farm such as Nodoroma (small, that is, in comparison to some of the huge racing farms), the job line distinctions are blurred so everyone has a chance to work in every area of the farm. In fact, it is a necessity that they be able to do so. If you are good and talented and persevere, you can conceivably start as a groom and work your way up to stud manager, trainer, or farm manager.

Mrs. Murch maintained that becoming a farm or stud manager is difficult at best for women. The general consensus is that handling stallions requires a man's strength, as do many of the other back-breaking aspects of farm management. Offhand, I could think of several women whose strength and talent would cause me to disagree, but Mrs. Murch's feeling is shared by the majority in the business.

Nodoroma had had some experience in hiring young women straight out of school who wanted to work with horses. After a period of time working as grooms they became discouraged. They decided that this wasn't quite the life they had thought it would be and left. I knew the type. I had seen many young women who had little practical experience with horses come into stables asking for a job as a groom. Idealistically they think it would be wonderful to "be around horses all day," without taking into account the tiring physical labor involved in mucking out stalls, and feeding, cleaning, and grooming a string of horses day after day.

For the women who want to do more than just groom, Mrs. Murch suggested some of the larger breeding farms. There, where jobs are more specialized, you could work as a brood-mare and foal groom and handler, or, if it is a racing farm, as an exercise rider. If you are talented enough, and have the experience, you could possibly find work as an assistant trainer.

In general, as we've seen in most areas, the "entry-level" or beginning job for those with little or no previous horse-related experience is a groom. Or in some cases you can start as an exercise rider. It is hard work, but on the right farm these jobs can lead to the kind of experience that will make you eligible for more responsibilities later on.

Horse breeding farms are located across the country, but the heavy concentrations are in Kentucky, Virginia, Maryland, Florida, and California. At a glance the picture-book beauty and tranquility of a breeding farm with its acres of rolling green pastures containing placidly grazing mares and frolicking long-legged foals is enough to tempt anyone into considering a life with horses. But for others the tranquility might prove to be too much of a good thing. Perhaps the best plan would be to arrange a part-time summer job to discover if life on a breeding farm is right for you.

14
Going by the Book:
Courses on Horses

Is a college degree or a course certificate a requirement to work in the horse industry today? Yes and no. The horse business used to be learned strictly through an apprentice system, and that is still possible. However, courses in horse and stable management, breeding, nutrition, and other subjects can expose you to knowledge and techniques it might take years to learn on the job. Graduates of these programs still usually have to start near the bottom of the ladder, but they have a broad view of the industry and an advantage over the competition.

If you are determined to make a career of horses, and want the extra edge a formal education can provide, a number of options are available. You may earn an instructor's certificate from a riding school, gain a horse-related bachelor's degree in a college program, or take a short vocational course for a specific job such as breeding farm groom or veterinarian technician. Following is a sampling of horse-related courses.

Certificate Courses

A certificate from a recognized riding school can go a long way toward getting you your first job, but there is no guarantee. Most schools maintain an active placement service and do their best, including giving advice on writing a resume, to help you land a job.

Pacific Horse Center in Elk Grove, California, offers three courses of study, each approximately twelve weeks long: Assistant Instructor, Instructor, and Riding Master. The minimum age for enrollment in the Assistant Instructor program is seventeen. Applicants must be able to ride at the walk, trot, and canter, and jump a small fence.

Students are taught the basic riding techniques of hunter seat equitation, dressage, show jumping, and cross-country riding. A horse is assigned to your care for the duration of the course, but you are required to ride many different horses to develop versatility as a rider. You may bring your own horse at no extra charge, provided the horse is capable of the work required. If not, there is a charge for boarding. Once you have mastered your basic position and riding technique, you are taught the principles of instruction through lectures, demonstrations, and films. You will later practice-teach and give "lecturettes" under the supervision of your instructor.

In addition to the riding and teaching, students study practical horse and stable management which focuses on such basic procedures as cleaning stalls, grooming, tack care, bandaging, and trailering. Other studies in the theory of horse management include nutrition, the horse in health and illness, lameness, and an introduction to breeding.

The school claims that graduates of its Assistant Instructor course will be able to manage a small stable or act as assistant to the manager of a larger one. You will also be able to teach beginner riders and assist in instructing advanced students.

131

The Instructor course is limited to graduates of the Assistant Instructor program, or to those who have obtained an equivalent certificate at another major riding school.

Students in this course are assigned two horses: a schooled horse capable of being shown, and a green horse to be trained under supervision. Some competitive riding in dressage and jumping is expected and field trips, guest lectures, and special clinics are also part of the training.

The course is designed to further the instruction begun in the Assistant Instructor program in horse and rider training, stable management, and treatment of disease. It is geared for students who are seriously considering the equestrian field as a career. To this end, the school offers instruction in the types of careers available and the earning potentials of each. Some of the areas covered are horse show management, course design, judging, and horse-related business management and record keeping. Depending on your field of interest, the school will actively assist you in finding a suitable position as an assistant trainer, instructor, stable manager, or professional rider.

The Riding Master course is designed for those who wish to pursue a career as a head instructor, stable manager, trainer, or stable owner. Competitive riding is required in your speciality. You will be assigned two horses to train, and given specific pupils to instruct. Students participate in the daily management functions of running a stable, and are given comprehensive training in the complete riding school operation—everything from advertising and soliciting pupils to record keeping and handling money and parents.

Graduates are actively assisted in finding jobs in the horse industry; you are also encouraged to call on the director and staff for continuing consultation if you wish to set up a business of your own.

Meredith Manor in Waverly, West Virginia, offers a similar three-level program: Assistant Instructor, Riding Instructor, and Riding Master or Riding-Blacksmith. A high school diploma or its equivalent is required for admission. You have a choice of riding majors—English, Western, or Versatility, which is a combination of English, Western, and saddle seat. You will study riding and training techniques, stable management, teaching methods, judging, showmanship, economics and general management, and show mastership—which means competing in your field of interest.

The twelve-week Assistant Instructor course prepares you to instruct beginner lessons, groom horses, and assist in managing a small stable. Graduates of the twenty-four-week Riding Instructor course are able to instruct and plan advanced lessons, and manage a horse operation. In the thirty-six-week Riding Master course you are prepared to school horses for competitive and pleasure riding, to evaluate and manage a horse facility, and to instruct group and private lessons. The Riding-Blacksmith course, also thirty-six weeks, offers comprehensive instruction in general and corrective shoeing.

In a unique program, Meredith Manor also offers a full Bachelor of Science degree in equestrian studies by combining the Riding Master or Riding-Blacksmith course (which make up your Junior and Senior years) with nearby Salem College's two-year liberal arts program. You may earn the degree in any of three ways: attend Salem College followed by Meredith Manor; attend Meredith Manor followed by Salem College; or attend Salem College in the fall and spring terms and Meredith Manor in the summer terms.

College Programs

A growing number of two- and four-year colleges and universities offer horse-related courses.

In response to the great demand for qualified riding instructors, and to help prepare students for careers in horse breeding and stable management, Southern Seminary Junior College for women in Buena Vista, Virginia, offers a Horsemanship Certificate. This program is combined with an approved college major—General Studies, Physical Education, Animal Science, or the Junior College Certificate—for the degree. The eight-course, twenty-two-credit-hour program consists of: stable management; the principles, theory, and fundamentals of riding and schooling; horse show management; evaluating and training green horses for riding, hunting, and showing; and practice teaching and business management.

During the two-year course of study you compete in and help run horse shows, hunter trials, and other horse events. The facilities consist of a sixty-four-horse stable, an indoor arena, an outdoor ring, and cross-country trails.

Not all degree programs are riding oriented. Minnesota Technical College in Waseca offers a Light Horse Management degree. This is a breeding and horse management-oriented, two-year program that gives an Associate of Arts degree in animal science with a horse management major. Courses required in the program are agriculture, biology, business, and communications. You then choose forty-one hours of horse courses from such subjects as livestock evaluation, light horse management, stable management, animal nutrition, Western or English equitation, young horse care and training, and farrier science. The program includes field trips to farms, clinics by professionals, and one semester spent on-the-job at a breeding or training farm.

The University of Arizona at Tucson offers a unique Race Track Management program that was initiated in 1974 in cooperation with the racing establishment. The purpose of the four-year degree course is to provide skilled personnel capable of handling positions in racetrack management and administration.

Students in this program take four required racetrack courses and some business courses as well as those already required for a B.S. degree in Agriculture with an animal science major. The four courses are: breeds and registry associations, organization and administration of animal racing facilities (both equine and canine), animal racing laws and enforcement, and current topics in racing.

In addition to these four courses, one semester is spent in the Internship Program in which you earn college credit while working at a recognized track or stud farm. The University will assist you in finding a job when you graduate, and has been successful in placing graduates at Los Alamitos, Bay Meadows, Delaware Park, The Jockey Club, Gainsway Farm, Oakland Park, Keeneland, and Arlington Park.

Vocational Training
One of the most well-respected vocational schools is the

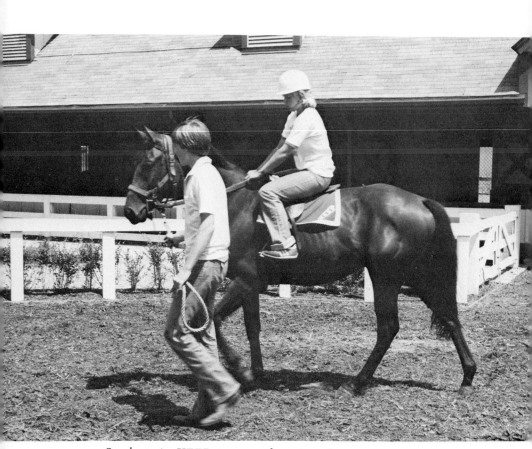

Students in KEEP program learning the ropes

Kentucky Equine Educational Program (KEEP) in Lexington. Organized several years ago to supply a trained work force for Kentucky's horse breeding, training, and racing industry, KEEP trains students to enter one of seven occupations: hotwalker, track groom, exercise rider, Standardbred caretaker, farm hand, farm groom, and foaling attendant.

Students enroll in the Thoroughbred Track, Standardbred Track, or Horse Farm Program. Thoroughbred

136

and Standardbred students learn stable care, grooming, nutrition, anatomy, health management, bandaging, and breaking. Farm students learn about breeding, foaling, nutrition, health care, and sales preparation.

The first three months are spent in a general course of study which is taught through lectures, demonstrations, and field trips. After three months you move into your career speciality. Prospective exercise riders begin galloping; hotwalkers begin to work with racehorses, walking hots; foaling attendants take part in farm activities caring for mares and foals. Six months is the average length of the course, but it is open-ended—you graduate when you have reached an employable level. After you have reached an acceptable level of skill, KEEP will help place you at a recognized track or breeding farm.

Applicants must be sixteen years old and complete the General Aptitude Test Battery (GATB) which is given at most public employment offices nationwide. Students who wish to train as exercise riders must show riding ability which will be tested the first week of school. There is usually a waiting list for admission and preference is given to Kentucky residents.

Veterinary technician training is taught in both vocational schools and through degree programs. Northwest College in Seattle has a nine-month vocational program which includes course work in anatomy and physiology, small animal behavior and care, large animal management and restraint, surgical assisting for large and small animals, anesthesiology, hematology, x-ray, urinalysis, pharmacology, and office procedures. Students must be high school graduates or have an equivalency diploma.

As you can see, you can take courses to learn how to do everything from design a show course to manage a stable or nail on a shoe. I have purposely omitted fees here since they vary widely and are constantly changing. To give you an idea of expenses, a course in veterinary technician training may cost $2,000 while the fees for a riding instructor certificate course might be $4,600. Contact the schools directly for accurate and up-to-date information on their fees and expenses. Also worth looking into: some schools offer working pupil programs for students who cannot afford the full fee.

To make the most of your education, narrow your field and know what you want to do, then evaluate the schools carefully. Investigate as many options as possible before making your decisions. You will find a listing of schools offering horse courses in the Appendix.

Glossary

AID   Any of the signals used by a rider to give instructions to the horse.

Artificial Aids: Items such as whips, spurs, and martingales used to help convey instructions to the horse.

Natural Aids: The body, hands, legs and voice as used by the rider to give instructions to the horse.

ARTIFICIAL INSEMINATION   The deposition of spermatozoa in the female genitalia by artificial rather than natural means.

BACKSTRETCH   The part of the racetrack farthest from the grandstand, opposite and parallel to the homestretch. Also commonly used to refer to the entire racing compound which includes barns, training tracks, living quarters and so on.

BREEZE   A controlled workout over a relatively short distance in which the horse is asked to approach racing speeds.

BUCKED SHIN   An inflammation of the cannon bone in the lower leg caused by stress; a common ailment among young racehorses.

CLAIMER   A horse entered in a claim race.

CLAIM RACE   A race in which all the horses are entered at stated prices and may be claimed (purchased) by any other owner of a starter in the race. In effect, all horses in a claim race are offered for sale.

COLIC   A general term which refers to pain in the abdomen.

COLLECTION   Shortening the pace by a light contact from the rider's hands and a steady pressure with the legs to make the horse flex its neck, relax its jaw and bring its hocks well under it so that it is properly balanced.

CONFORMATION   The formation and arrangements of the parts of the horse.

CUTTING HORSE   A horse specially trained for separating selected cattle from a herd.

DRAG HUNT   A hunt staged on horseback with hounds following a laid trail made by dragging a bag of anise seed or litter from a fox's den.

DRESSAGE   The art of training horses to perform all movements in a balanced, supple, obedient and attentive manner. Dressage competitions are divided into levels of training and involve a specific set of movements designed to test the proficiency of horse and rider.

ENGLISH SADDLE   Characterized by a relatively flat seat and light weight, types of English saddles are modified specifically for pleasure riding, racing, jumping, and polo.

ENGLISH SEAT   Using an English, or "flat" saddle, the rider sits forward in the saddle with the knees bent, heels down, ankles flexed in and the calf of the leg touching the horse, and slightly behind the girth. The reins are carried in both hands. The rider's eyes should be looking up and the shoulders back. At the walk and slow trot, the body is vertical with the seat in the saddle; at the posting trot, the body should incline forward rising with the motion of the trot. At the canter, the body should be halfway between posting trot and walk, and when galloping and jumping, it should have the same forward inclination as at the posting trot.

EQUITATION CLASS   A competition in the art of riding. The competition is judged solely on the horsemanship of the rider with categories according to age, experience, previous winnings and type of riding.

EVENTING   Refers to three-day horse trials. The first day of competition is dressage; the second day endurance—roads and tracks, steeplechase and cross-country; the third day is stadium jumping.

FLOAT   To file down with a dental rasp teeth which have grown into uneven points.

FOAL   A young, unweaned horse of either sex.

FOUNDER *(Laminitis)*   A painful ailment caused by congested blood in the legs and feet. The laminae tissue inside the hoof become inflamed and swell up; unchecked, it can cause permanent crippling and even death.

FURLONG   One-eighth of a mile (201.17 meters).

GAITED HORSES   Three-gaited and five-gaited horses are members of the American Saddle Horse breed. Three-gaited horses perform at the walk, trot and canter, with high, animated action in front and behind at the trot. Five-gaited horses also do the slow gait, a stepping gait performed slowly with animated and high action, and the rack, a four-beat gait in which each hoof strikes the ground separately and at regular intervals. The rack is performed at speed and with great brilliance.

GELD   To cut or castrate a male horse.

GELDING   A castrated male horse.

GIRTH   A band of leather, cotton cord or canvas that buckles or ties to the saddle and fits around the belly of the horse to hold the saddle in place.

GREEN   A young horse, or a horse whose schooling is incomplete.

GYMKHANA   Mounted games featuring novelty contests such as spearing rings, musical chairs and bareback jumping.

HACK   A horse used for ordinary pleasure riding; a horse that is kept exclusively for hire.

HAND   A unit of measure equal to four inches, used to determine the height of a horse. Horses are measured from the ground to the withers.

HUNTER   A horse trained and kept for hunting; a horse shown in hunter classes.

HUNTER CLASS   A competition in which the horses are judged on their manners, jumping performance, style and soundness. The obstacles are built to look natural and similar to those found in hunting.

HUNTING   The sport of following hounds on horseback in pursuit of a live quarry or following an artifically laid trail (drag hunt).

JUMPER CLASS   A competition in which the horse is judged solely on his ability to jump.

JUNIOR   A rider under the age of eighteen.

LAMINITIS (see *Founder*).

LEAD SHANK   A long strap made of leather, nylon or cotton rope with a snap on one end that attaches to the halter for leading or tying the horse.

LET DOWN   A horse taken off an exercise or training program and allowed to return to a relaxed, out-of-condition state.

142

LONGEING   The act of exercising a horse in a circle on the end of a longe rein.

LONGE REIN   A strong, light strap, usually made of webbing or leather about twenty-five to thirty feet long, one end of which is attached by a swiveled snap to the noseband of the caveson or halter.

NAVICULAR DISEASE   An inflammation of the small navicular bone of the front feet which may result in lameness. The symptoms may be eliminated by corrective shoeing or by a relatively simple operation known as nerving.

PADDOCK   A grassy enclosure in which horses can be turned out; the enclosure at a racetrack in which the horses are paraded and then mounted before a race.

PASTERN   The part of the horse's leg between the fetlock joint and the hoof; it should slope about 45° and should be neither too long nor too short.

POSTING TROT   The trot is a two-beat gait. When posting, the rider rises at one beat and sits at the next. This rising and descending of the rider with the rhythm of the trot reduces the shock or jar of the trot for both horse and rider.

POULTICE   A soft, usually heated and sometimes medicated mass spread on cloth and applied to the legs.

RACE MEETING   A period of time, usually several weeks, during which a set number of races are held at a particular track.

RANK   Slang term used to refer to a difficult, unruly horse.

SADDLE SEAT   The position assumed when riding a three- or five-gaited horse. The rider sits erect and well back in the saddle, with the hands slightly elevated.

SCRATCH   To withdraw a horse from a race, or other equestrian event, after it has been officially entered.

SHEDROW   A covered walking area, usually attached to the barn and in front of the stall area.

SOUND   A horse free from defects, with perfect sight and hearing, good heart and lungs, and who is not lame or possessed of a condition that may lead to lameness.

STAKES RACE   Short for sweepstakes. Each owner puts up an equal amount of money, with the track putting up additional money. The sum is then divided between the first four horses.

STEEPLECHASE   A race of European origin from two to three miles long with ten to thirty jumps or hurdles. It is a combination of running on the turf and jumping.

STIRRUP   The part of the saddle on which the rider's foot is placed. Heavy wooden stirrups are used on Western saddles, and light metal stirrups are used on English saddles.

TACK   The equipment that is used on or attached to riding and driving horses, such as the saddle, bridle, or harness. *To tack up:* To put the saddle and bridle, or other equipment, on the horse.

WESTERN SADDLE   Characterized by a comparatively deep seat with heavy square or round "skirts," the Western saddle is designed to give comfort for all day riding and is strong enough to stand up under the strain of calf roping. Its usual weight is between 35 and 40 pounds.

WESTERN SEAT   The rider uses a stock, or Western saddle, and sits straight, keeping the legs fairly straight. The balls of the feet rest on the stirrup treads, heels down. The reins are carried in the left hand in a relaxed manner, with the hand slightly above and ahead of the horn. The right hand should be placed on the thigh, or dropped loosely at the side, or held about waist high without resting on anything. "Sitting" in the saddle is required at all gaits. Neither posting at the trot (jog) nor standing in the stirrups at the trot or gallop (lope) is accepted.

WITHERS   The highest part of the horse's back; the area at the base of the neck between the shoulder blades.

YEARLING   A young horse of either sex between the ages of one and two years.

Appendix

Colleges and Universities Offering Equine Courses

The following listing is provided by the American Horse Council. They also suggest that you contact the land grant university in your state for information on available horse programs and for assistance in locating other schools in the state offering equine courses.

Auburn University
Auburn, AL 36830

Arizona State University
Tempe, AZ 85281

Prescott College
Prescott, AZ 86301

Scottsdale Community
College
Scottsdale, AZ 85251

University of Arizona
Tucson, AZ 85721

Arkansas State University
State University, AK 72467

University of Arkansas
Fayetteville, AK 72701

California Polytechnic State
University
San Luis Obispo, CA 93401

California State University
Chico, CA 95926

California State Polytechnic
University
Pomona, CA 91768

Fresno State College
Fresno, CA 93721

Univ. of California
Davis, CA 95616

Colorado State University
Fort Collins, CO 80523

Lamar Community College
Lamar, CO 81052

University of Connecticut
Storrs, CT 06268

Delaware Technical &
   Community College
Northern Branch
Wilmington, DE 19899

University of Delaware
Newark, DE 19711

Santa Fe Community College
Gainesville, FL 32611

University of Florida
Gainesville, FL 32611

University of Georgia
Athens, GA 30602

University of Idaho
Moscow, ID 83843

Belleville Area College
Belleville, IL 62220

University of Illinois
Urbana, IL 61801

Ball State University
Muncie, IN 47306

Purdue University
West Lafayette, IN 47907

Iowa State University
Ames, IA 50010

Kirkwood Community
   College
Cedar Rapids, IA 52401

Kansas State University
Manhattan, KS 66502

Morehead State University
Morehead, KY 40351

Murray State University
Murray, KY 42071

University of Kentucky
Lexington, KY 40506

Louisiana State University
Baton Rouge, LA 70803

Louisiana Tech University
Ruston, LA 71270

McNeese State College
Lake Charles, LA 70609

Southeastern Louisiana Univ.
Hammond, LA 70402

University of Maine
Orono, ME 04473

University of Maryland
College Park, MD 20742

Mt. Holyoke College
South Hadley, MA 01075

University of Massachusetts
Amherst, MA 01003

Cheff Center
Augusta, MI 04330

Michigan State University
East Lansing, MI 48824

University of Minnesota
   Technical College
Crookston, MN 56716

University of Minnesota
Waseca, MN 56093

Mississippi State University
Mississippi State, MS 39762

The Lindenwood Colleges
St. Charles, MO 63301

Stephens College
Columbia, MO 65201

University of Missouri
Columbia, MO 65201

William Woods College
Fulton, MO 65251

Montana State University
Bozeman, MT 59715

University of Nebraska
Lincoln, NB 68588

University of New
  Hampshire
Durham, NH 03824

Centenary College
Hackettstown, NJ 07840

Rutgers University/Cook
  College
New Brunswick, NJ 08903

Bennet College
Millbrook, NY 12545

Cazenovia College
Cazenovia, NY 13035

Cornell University
Ithaca, NY 14850

State University of New York
Alfred, NY 14802

State University of New York
Canton, NY 13617

State University of New York
Cobeskill, NY 12043

State University of New York
Delhi, NY 13753

State University of New York
Morrisville, NY 13408

North Carolina State
  University
Raleigh, NC 27607

North Dakota State
  University
Fargo, ND 58102

Findlay College
Findlay, OH 45840

Lake Erie College
Painesville, OH 44077

Ohio State University
Columbus, OH 43210

Eastern Oklahoma State
  College
Wilburton, OK 74578

Northwestern Oklahoma
  State University
Alva, OK 73717

Oklahoma State University
Stillwater, OK 74074

Panhandle State University
Goodwell, OK 73939

Oregon State University
Corvallis, OR 97331

Pennsylvania State University
University Park, PA 16820

University of Rhode Island
Kingston, RI 02881

Clemson University
Clemson, SC 29631

Black Hills State College
Spearfish, SD 57783

South Dakota State University
Brookings, SD 57006

Middle Tennessee State
University
Murfreesboro, TN 37132

University of Tennessee
Knoxville, TN 37916

Texas A & M University
College Station, TX 77843

West Texas State University
Canyon, TX 79016

University of Vermont
Burlington, VT 05401

Blue Ridge Community
College
Weyers Cave, VA 24486

Lord Fairfax Community
College
Middleton, VA 22645

Southern Junior Seminary
Buena Vista, VA 24416

Virginia Intermont College
Bristol, VA 24201

Virginia Polytechnic Institute
and State University
Blacksburg, VA 24060

Olympia Vocational Technical
Institute
Olympia, WA 98501

Washington State University
Pullman, WA 99164

West Virginia University
Morgantown, WV 26505

University of Wisconsin
River Falls, WI 54022

Northwest Community
College
Powell, WY 82435

Farrier Schools

The following public and private schools offer farrier instruction. Questions about any phase of the farrier's trade may be directed to the American Farrier's Association, P.O. Box 695, Albuquerque, NM 87103.

Tucson School of
Horseshoeing
2111 E. Benson Highway
Tucson, AZ 85714

Western School of
Horseshoeing
2801 S. Maryland Avenue
Phoenix, AZ 85017

150

California State Polytechnic University
3801 W. Temple Avenue
Pomona, CA 91768

California State Polytechnic University
San Luis Obispo, CA 93401

Merced Community College
Dept. of Agriculture
Merced, CA 95340

Porterville Horseshoeing School
810 N. Jaye Street
Porterville, CA 93257

Santa Cruz Horseshoeing School
772 Buena Vista Drive
Watsonville, CA 95076

T-Bone Horseshoeing School
Calabasas, CA 91302

Valley Vocational Center
15359 Proctor Avenue
City of Industry, CA 91744

Colorado Northwestern Community College
School of Horseshoeing
Box 9010
Steamboat Springs, CO 80477

Hillcraft School of Horseshoeing
10890 Dear Creek Canyon Road
Littleton, CO 80120

Warrington's School of Horseshoeing
Townsend, DE 19734

Southeastern School of Horseshoeing
Route 5
Canton, GA 30114

Midwest Horseshoeing School
Maple Lane Road
Rural Route 3
Macomb, IL 61455

Kirkwood Community College
Agribusiness & Natural Resources
Box 2068
Cedar Rapids, IA 52406

Tri-State Farrier's School
26 Charemoor
Sibley, IA 51249

Kansas Horseshoeing School
Route 1, Box 33
Girard, KS 66743

Kentucky School of Horseshoeing
Box 12031
Lexington, KY 40511

New England Farrier's School
Raymond, ME 04071

University of Maine
Extension Livestock Specialist
332 Hitchner Hall
Orono, ME 14473

Horses A to Z, Inc.
Leelaunau Schools
Glen Arbor, MI 49636

Michigan School of Horseshoeing
Box 423
Belleville, MI 48111

151

Wolverine Farrier School
7690 Wiggins Road
Howell, MI 48843

Anoka Area Vocational
  Technical Institute
Box 191
Anoka, MN 55303

South Central Missouri
  School of Horseshoeing
Route 2, Box 292
West Plains, MO 65775

Montana State University
Dept. of Animal & Range
  Science & Continuing
  Education
Bozeman, MT 59715

Nebraska Farrier School, Inc.
R.D. No. 1
Denton, NE 68339

South Jersey School of
  Horseshoeing
R.D. Box 126
Mullica Hill, NJ 08062

New Mexico State University
P.O. Box 3501
Las Cruces, NM 88003

Eastern States Farrier School
R.D. 1, Box 49
Phoenix, NY 13135

Horses A to Z, Inc.
State University of New York
Cobbeskill, NY 12043

North Carolina School of
  Horseshoeing
Rt. 1, Box 343
Pleasant Grove, NC 27313

Pitt Technical Institute
P.O. Drawer 7007
Greenville, NC 27834

Oklahoma Horseshoeing
  School
Route 1, Box U-26
Stillwater, OK 74074

Oklahoma Farriers College
Route 1, Box 13
Sperry, OK 74073

Oklahoma State Horseshoeing
  School
Route 1, Box 28-B
Ardmore, OK 73401

Misty Oaks Farrier School
3603 Leland Road
Sun Valley, OR 97478

Oregon State University
Corvalis, OR 97331

Rogue Community College
3345 Redwood Pass Highway
Grants Pass, OR 97526

Harold Musselman
  Horseshoeing School
R.D. 1
Dillsburg, PA 17019

Pennsylvania State University
College of Agriculture
University Park, PA 16802

Middle Tennessee State
University
College of Agriculture
Box 269
Murfreesboro, TN 37132

Mid-South School of
Horseshoeing
4964 Getwell
Memphis, TN 38118

Hyatt School of Horseshoeing
Box 232-A
Pottsboro, TX 75076

North Texas Farriers School
P.O. Box 666
Mineral Wells, TX 76067

North Texas Horseshoeing
Institute
821 E. Southlake Blvd.
Grapevine, TX 76051

Sul Ross State University
Alpine, TX 79830

Texoma Horseshoeing School
Route 1
Pottsboro, TX 75076

Utah State University
Conference & Inst. Division
Logan, UT 84322

Martinsville School of
Farriery
P.O. Box 1341
Martinsville, VA 24112

Olympia Technical
Community College
2011 Mottman Road, SW
Olympia, WA 98502

Meredith Manor
Rt. 1, Box 76
Waverly, WV 26184

University of Wisconsin
College of Agriculture
River Falls, WI 54022

Central Wyoming College
Dean of Special Services
Riverton, WY 82501

Canadian National School of
Horseshoeing
Box 1203
Uxbridge, Ontario
CANADA

Olds Regional College
Olds, Alberta
CANADA TOM1PO

The Smithy
Thornton Hough
Wirral
Chrsire, ENGLAND

Colleges of Veterinary Medicine

School of Veterinary Medicine
Auburn University
Auburn, AL 36803

School of Veterinary Medicine
Tuskegee Institute
Tuskegee, AL 36088

School of Veterinary Medicine
University of California
Davis, CA 95616

College of Veterinary
Medicine and Biomedical
Sciences
Colorado State University
Fort Collins, CO 80521

College of Veterinary
Medicine
University of Georgia
Athens, GA 30601

College of Veterinary
Medicine
University of Illinois
Urbana, IL 61801

School of Veterinary Medicine
Purdue University
West Lafayette, IN 47907

College of Veterinary
Medicine
Iowa State University
Ames, IA 50010

College of Veterinary
Medicine
Kansas State University
Manhattan, KS 66502

College of Veterinary
Medicine
Louisiana State University
Baton Rouge, LA 70803

College of Veterinary
Medicine
Michigan State University
East Lansing, MI 48823

College of Veterinary
Medicine
University of Minnesota
St. Paul, MN 55101

College of Veterinary
Medicine
University of Missouri
Columbia, MO 65202

New York State Veterinary
College
Cornell University
Ithaca, NY 14850

College of Veterinary
Medicine
Ohio State University
Columbus, OH 43210

College of Veterinary
Medicine
Oklahoma State University
Stillwater, OK 74074

School of Veterinary Medicine
University of Pennsylvania
Philadelphia, PA 19104

College of Veterinary
Medicine
Texas A & M University
College Station, TX 77843

College of Veterinary
Medicine
Washington State University
Pullman, WA 99163

Ontario Veterinary College
University of Guelph
Guelph, Ontario
CANADA

École de Médecine Vétérinaire
Université de Montréal
St. Hyacinthe, Québec
CANADA

Western College of Veterinary
   Medicine
University of Saskatchewan
Saskatoon, Saskatchewan
CANADA

Veterinary Technician Training

Abraham Baldwin
   Agricultural College
ABAC Station
Tifton, GA 31794

Colby Community College
Colby, KS 67701

Camden County Community
   College
Little Gloucester Road
Blackwood, NJ 08012

Agricultural Technology
   Division
Lee County Incorporated
   Education Center
Sanford, NC 27330

Ft. Steilacoom Community
   College
6010 Mt. Tacoma Drive, SW
Tacoma, WA 98499

Northwest College
1305 Seneca Street
Seattle, WA 98101

Centralia College of
   Agriculture Technology
Huron Park, Ontario
CANADA

Western Ontario Agriculture
   School
Ridgetown, Ontario
CANADA

Vocational Schools

Kentucky Equine Education
   Program
P.O. Box 11188
Lexington, KY 40511

International School of
   Harness Racing
P.O. Box 978—Barn 75
Roosevelt Raceway
Westbury, L. I., NY 11590

L.A. Wilson Technological
   Center
Thoroughbred Care &
   Training Program
Dix Hills, L. I., NY 11746

Orange County Board of
   Cooperative Educational
   Services (BOCES)
Gibson Road
Goshen, NY 10924

Mon Ami Le Cheval
Box 462
Malvern Hill, PA 19355

Meredith Manor
Route 1, Box 76
Waverly, WV 26184

Directory of Certificate Courses

Pacific Horse Center
P. O. Box L
Elk Grove, CA 95624

Potomac Horse Center
14211 Quince Orchard Road
Gaithersburg, MD 20760

Fulmer International School
of Equitation, Inc.
Prescott Street
Pepperell, MA 01463

Flintlock Farm Equestrian
Center
Box 396
Ontonagon, MI 49953

Cherry Meadow Farm
1072 Pulaski Road
E. Northport, L.I., NY
11731

Buttonwood Combined
Training Center
Hollow Road
Birchrunville, PA 19421

Fox Hollow Farm
Yellow Springs Road
Chester Springs, PA 19425

Pen-Y-Bryn Equestrian
Center, Ltd.
Seven Oaks Road
Chester Springs, PA 19425

Pleasant Hollow Farms
R.D. 1, Box 481
Coopersburg, PA 18036

Wonderland Farms
R.D. 5
West Chester, PA 19380

Morven Park International
Equestrian Institute
Leesburg, VA 22075

Whiting's Neck Equestrian
Centre
Route 3, Box 105D
Martinsburg, WV 25401

Meredith Manor
Route 1, Box 76
Waverly, WV 26184

Index

Index